Advance Praise

"This is the book I wish I had written but it found Sara Waters instead. Powerful. Moving. An essential read for those of us willing to do what it takes to evolve. Waters has personally answered the call to the heroine's journey, and this outstanding book gives the reader not only a path of practice but the courage and curiosity to try it too."

—SUNNI BROWN, bestselling author, TED speaker, and social entrepreneur at SB Ink and The Center for Deep Self Design

"Considering the state of the world today, this book is a welcome reminder to use more question marks. We are living in a moment when so many people can benefit from practicing more curiosity within themselves and with each other. Waters has not only given us the tools, but also the permission to become more curious so that we can know ourselves more, listen better, and heal our pain and divisions. When curiosity is pure, love will prevail."

—DR. KATIE DECKER, MsED, C.A.C.C.P, and CEO of 5280 Balanced Health Center

"My dear friend and mentor has created a roadmap that gently guides us through the fear of uncertainty toward a greater purpose. Whether you're hoping to more truly understand yourself, become a better communicator, expand your spiritual practice, or search for your life's meaning, More YourSELF will empower that pursuit by tapping into the power of your own innate sense of curiosity. Each chapter serves as loving navigation, helping you find your way home to yourself. I am forever grateful for Waters' wisdom and grateful her work is being shared on a larger stage."

—LAUREN GARDNER, MLB and NHL sportscaster, host and sideline reporter, and member of the history-making first MLB game ever broadcast by an all-woman team

MORE
YourSELF

MORE
YourSELF

QUESTION WHAT YOU THINK YOU KNOW
TO REALIZE WHO YOU ARE

—from the Mind of an Internal Family Systems Therapist

SARA WATERS, MA, LPC

LIONCREST
PUBLISHING

MORE YOURSELF
*Question What You Think You Know to Realize Who You Are—
from the Mind of an Internal Family Systems Therapist*

ISBN 978-1-5445-3656-9 *Hardcover*
      978-1-5445-3657-6 *Paperback*
      978-1-5445-3658-3 *Ebook*

Table
of
Contents

1 Section:

2

Section:
181 CONNECTION WITH OTHERS

3Section:

To my clients

and my crazy-makers

If you are reading this, one of three things may be true:

✓ Your life is not quite as you want it. It's a rare occasion when you feel like yourself. You are searching for guidance, a sign, or a set of tools to support some degree of change or a remembering of who you are.

The Gauntlet

✓ Someone who cares about you has recognized you may be living smaller than or out of alignment with what is possible for you. This book has been suggested or gifted to you.

✓ You've stumbled across this book unintentionally.

Whatever the case, I encourage you to keep reading. There are no coincidences. On this day and in this moment, this book is supposed to be in your hands.

I do not subscribe to the belief that the trajectories of our lives are already mapped out. I don't believe every decision we will ever make is already known. However, I have stepped fully into the belief that everything happens exactly as it's supposed to. I can look back through my life and notice that every single hardship, heartbreak, important conversation, death, win, epic failure, twist, turn, and reroute *had* to happen exactly as it did to lead me to where I stand today, which, if I do say so myself, is a pretty dope place to be. My life is far from perfect, but I feel a ton of joy nearly every day. I let go of the idea that things should be fair a long time ago. Significant sacrifices, my own and those of people I've loved very much, had to be made for my current reality to exist. This is true for you too. The sooner you accept it, the sooner you will be able to take a big ol' breath and begin taking steps, one at a time, into a new trajectory, where you'll feel more awake, more aware, more alive, and (the best part) so much more *yourself*.

This sounds like a big promise, doesn't it? I should give the caveat that I'm not a wizard. I don't consider myself to be enlightened. I don't think my IQ is likely even very high. But I am an expert at being human, just like you. We've been doing that every second of every minute since the day we were born.

In my professional life, I'm a psychotherapist and psychological wellness speaker. I own a private practice in Castle Rock, a cute little town just south of Denver, Colorado. I specialize in trauma reprocessing for teen and adult clients. Being a therapist, you'd think I'd have figured out a thing or two about how to stream-line life and dodge pain. In reality, it's no more of a cakewalk for me than it is for anyone else. I mess up all the damn time, and I have plenty of funky thoughts and big feelings that are not always pleasant. Sometimes I wish I didn't know so much about psychology. It would be nice to be ignorant to my own bullshit every once in a while.

The last ten years of my life have been a journey of waking up and figuring out who the hell I am. I used to roll my eyes at the term "authenticity" until I stopped to consider what it actually means and consequently discovered I was doing pretty much the opposite of what anyone would consider "authentic living." I felt like shit for a long time. I was angry, resentful, directionless, insecure, and convinced I'd been cheated by a raw deal. Until finally, I realized nobody was going to swoop in and save me. The superhero wasn't coming. If I wanted my life to stop sucking, it was up to me to change it.

Many of us have lost track of our identities. It happened slowly and subtly over time until we woke up one day, looked around, and realized these are not the lives we thought we'd be living. We think, "This is not the *me* I wanted to become." We didn't mean for it to get this way. It just happened. Ugh, that's an awful feeling. Waking up each day and settling for a life less than joy-filled is the ultimate self-sabotage. It's a perpetual hamster wheel of drama and struggle or, at best, incessant monotony. No frickin' thanks.

This is a book about introspection, change, growth, and forward movement *out* of that kind of stuckness. Unlike some books you'll find alongside it on the bookstore shelves, this one will not give you answers. I don't have them. Every piece of advice I could possibly give you would be colored by the lens of my own experiences, biases, beliefs, and agendas. Rather, I'm going to teach you some psychotherapeutic tricks of the trade to help you identify, observe, and desensitize your own triggers, strongholds, past wounds, and anything else that may be blocking clear access to your most authentic self. By flipping what I call "U-turns" with your attention, swerving its direction from outward to inward and becoming more engaged with the inner workings of your psyche, you'll learn how to create shift where change is needed and tap straight into your own infinite reservoir of clarity and intuition.

At the same time, this is a book about learning how to let go of your attachments to what you *think* you know in exchange for an infusion of curiosity. An old Chinese proverb says, "You cannot fill a cup that is already full." In order to receive, you must first unclench your fists and turn your palms up to the sky, open your mind, and surrender your grip on certainty.

Traveling through these chapters will require you to take a raw and honest inventory of your life. You will need to challenge your beliefs, thought patterns, and default behaviors and the implicit contracts and agreements you've made with yourself and others. Come to this content with a willingness to identify and break old patterns and swap them out for a new level of openness in your mind and heart. Ultimately, this is a journey of remembering your inherent curious nature and getting back to the business of functioning and feeling *like yourself.*

You'll notice as you read and do the work in this book that you'll start to feel more calm, level-headed, and compassionate (toward others as well as yourself). You'll be less reactive and more thoughtful. You'll feel clearer and more confident while becoming less busy-minded, judgmental, negative, and frantic. When you experience hardship, make mistakes, and fall flat on your face (which you will), you'll rebound more quickly and learn important lessons from the pain. You will feel like *you*. That kind of authenticity is the natural byproduct of an aligned life. Chapter by chapter, these pages will guide you through the process.

If you let it, this work will change your life forever. We feel pain and strife when we experience disconnection from ourselves, other people, and the big, beautiful world around us. Curiosity is the antidote to disconnection. It's the best kind of medicine. If you are willing to put in the work, these strategies and considerations can rehabilitate and rejuvenate connection.

Albert Einstein once famously said, "I have no special talents. I am only passionately curious." Curiosity will open your mind, nurture the dry and frozen ground, and facilitate the exploration and discovery of wonderful things. We are all born with an inherent sense of curiosity. Those of us with addictions to certainty, however, have forgotten how to use it. An inquisitive person is an awake person. When we are awake, we grow. As we grow, we shed everything that no longer serves us, and we move forward with better direction and a clearer purpose.

This pursuit is not for the faint of heart. There is perhaps no scarier work than challenging our own (potentially outdated or unhealthy) default thoughts, choices, behaviors, and reactions. Be encouraged: if even small concepts from this book resonate and feel usable, you'll notice a palpable shift. My hope is that you take away from this book what feels helpful, true, and good right now. Over time, this is the kind of book that welcomes you to return again and again, absorbing more as you continue to awaken and grow.

In his book *My Grandmother's Hands,* about the relation-ship between trauma and racism, Resmaa Menakem writes about clean pain and dirty pain. He describes clean pain as the temporary discomfort associated with shaking things up and changing patterns. It makes me think of every time I remove processed sugar from my diet. For the first couple weeks, everything sucks. I get headaches, I'm grouchy, and all I can think about is ice cream. Inside my mind, there's a raging boxing match between my healthy nutritional goals and the parts of me that want to justify my chronic sugar habit and cave in to the addiction. The struggle is brutal for at least four-teen days until I get over the hump. Then my tastebuds start to adapt and appreciate natural sugars more, and the inner street fight subsides. That's clean pain. At best, it is an imme-diate but temporary inconvenience for the sake of long-term betterment. At worst, it feels like full-blown withdrawal and an intense mind game between my goals and my own stub-bornness. Clean pain is a normal and necessary part of healthy evolution and holistic healing.

Dirty pain, as Menakem describes it, is neurotic and long lasting. When I get in a rut and stop exercising for a while, for example, I have a hard time mustering the motivation to get going again. I kick the can down the road with every justification and avoidance tactic I can think of. Sometimes, months will pass, creating stag-nation and an ever-increasing sense of blaaaah. I know what I want but choose to stay in the seemingly more comfortable space of complacency, staring at my sneakers, as if daydreaming about feeling physically fit will make it so. I waste time saving Instagram posts and fitness inspiration on Pinterest, then tell myself I'll get started tomorrow. Until tomorrow becomes today, and the cycle of dirty pain continues.

Reading this book is like strapping on your workout shoes and stepping out onto the running trail. Considering these concepts and putting them into practice are your way out of the dirty pain created by complacency. Clean pain involves getting out of your comfort zone. But dirty pain is incessant and can be never-ending.

The following ten agreements are critical to the mission of this book. We are looking for a "yes" (or at least an "I am willing to try") response to each statement. Read them and notice your internal reaction to each:

✓ I value meaningful connection (with myself and others) *over* being right or staying comfortable.

✓ I have hope there is more capacity for joy and abundance within myself, my relationships, and the world around me than what I am currently experiencing.

✓ I respect and accept that there is so much I do not know or understand. I am open and ready to learn.

✓ I recognize discomfort is a natural component of growth, and I embrace this as part of the process. I am willing to get vulnerably uncomfortable.

✓ I recognize my beliefs, opinions, needs, and wants are no more and no less valuable than those of any other person or group of people.

✓ I accept it is possible my current perceptions, beliefs, opinions, and behaviors are causing unhappiness and potentially harm to myself or others.

✓ I recognize what I think I know might be faulty. I am willing to challenge my current perceptions, beliefs, opinions, and behaviors for the sake of personal expansion and the benefit of everything and everyone I engage with.

✓ I am willing to explore and consider things from my past (wounds, experiences, teachings, norms, cultural and societal schemas, and messaging) that may currently be blocking me from feeling and functioning authentically.

✓ I recognize perfection does not exist. I give myself permission to make mistakes, move forward with an eternal learner's mind, and forever be a work in progress.

✓ I accept certainty *is not real* and my reliance on it will hold me back and keep me stuck. I am willing to welcome uncertainty and trust I can be okay as I step into it.

There you go. The gauntlet has been thrown, and you are invited to step into the arena. How are you feeling? A little (or a lot) afraid to turn the page and start diving in but interested enough to give it a go?

Okay then. Let's get this party started.

This book is divided into three sections. The first (biggest and possibly most important) section will introduce and explore the use of mindful introspection and curiosity within and about yourself.

The second section will guide you toward more healthy and meaningful interpersonal connections by increasing your curiosity about other people.

Finally, the third section will take a look at how and why introspection and a pure and active sense of curiosity matter in the grand scheme of your lifetime, your place and purpose in the world, and the scope of existential exploration. Each section builds on the one before. By the time you reach the last page, you will be tapped right back into your intuition, complemented by the bold, brilliant source of natural inquisitiveness that you've always had within you but have perhaps lost touch with.

As you read, remember I am for you. I am with you. And I am just like you in countless ways. We are each just one small person, totally screwed up on so many levels. We are breathing, walking, talking, tangled-up balls of thoughts and feelings. It is chaotic, this whole "being human" thing. But maybe the mess is where the beauty lives and where the appreciation for the journey (more so than the destination) exists. Maybe our fundamental curiosity is what makes us special. Makes us alike. Makes us capable of evolving. Maybe our willingness to surrender to the unarguable fact that we don't have all the answers is what makes us brilliant.

Kinda like Einstein.

In the Harry Potter stories by J. K. Rowling, young wizards learn how to make Veritaserum, a potion that forces the drinker to answer any questions asked of them truthfully. After ingesting the truth serum, an individual loses the ability to respond in any way other than with sincere transparency and honesty. If I were a wizard, I would concoct Curioserum, a potion that disables the drinker's

Curiosity—
An Invitation

biases and attachments to certainty, allowing their natural sense of curiosity to flow in abundance. I would mass produce it in capsule form and sell it in bulk with a recommendation to ingest it upon waking every morning. I would make sure it had extended-release qualities too so it wouldn't peter out by the end of the day.

We hear all the time that our bodies are composed mostly of water. Every competent medical professional says that staying hydrated is a fundamental part of our biological wellness. The same can, and arguably should, be said about the role of curiosity in our psychological wellness. Our psychological system is run by an innate desire to intake information and use that data to support our survival. In recent years, humans have come to appreciate the role of curiosity not only for basic survival but also in the pursuit of creativity, innovation, connection, and productivity. We currently find ourselves in what some are calling the Psychological Era. We understand how important it is to observe, explore, understand, treat, heal, and support our psychological well-being. Among consumers who are on board for elevated psychological adeptness, my Curioserum would be a bestseller!

I'm not a wizard and don't have a pending patent or FDA approval on Curioserum. But not all hope is lost. Lucky for every single one of us, this very valuable sense of curiosity already lives inside all humans. You don't need a magic serum as long as you are willing to put in the work and commit to a practice of honing your already-existent sense of curiosity. It has been there within you since before you were even born. Studies of human development show our sense of implicit curiosity kicks in before eight weeks in utero, as our sensory receptors come online. You have been a curious being since shortly after your conception, as you grew inside your mother's belly.

Curiosity is a universal characteristic of infants and toddlers. Children, in general, have greater unbridled access to inquisitiveness than most adults. The unfortunate process of curiosity desensitization begins early in life as a result of natural consequences, in combination with the influences of those around us. A kid learns that touching a hot burner on the stove, for example, is never again worth being curious about. And the startling sound of a raised adult voice yelling "No!" when a child bites down on a grasshopper to see what it tastes like is enough to train that particular curiosity out of the child.

As we get older and our cognitive development evolves, two things happen that dampen our natural sense of curiosity. The first is our psychological system begins to equate uncertainty with risk and danger, teaching us the function of avoidance. In other words, if we can't accurately predict an outcome to a particular choice or behavior, we adapt by minimizing risk. We stick with what is familiar and known. For example, among my clients who choose to stay involved in physically abusive relationships, a common theme is the devil we know is often less scary than the devil we don't know. This causes people to refrain from seeking better circumstances, even if the current one totally sucks. Researchers now understand that on a neurobiological level, the brain and nervous system detect and read psychological distress similar to the way they interpret signals of pain from physical injury. Because of this, a resistance to curiosity—or preemptive avoidance of new pain—runs in the background of our subconscious. From a survivalist perspective, it makes a lot of sense to correlate avoidance with safety.

The second thing that fights against our inherent curiosity is the influences of projected fears from the people and cultures around us. It is impossible for any human to be without internal biases, judgments, and agendas. Our life experiences and the messaging we soak up from the folks and world around us color the way we think, believe, make choices, and react. Everyone experiences the world through a completely unique lens influenced by everything from our genetic predispositions to the way we were parented. Traumatic experiences play a huge role in the ways we function as we move through life. We are exposed to perspectives from our coaches, friends, teachers, neighbors, churches, and family members. Media incessantly thrusts posts in front of our faces in an attempt to convince us of one thing or another. It is not possible to dodge the impact of external influences no matter how hard we try. Because of this, we start to wrap ourselves in the warm blanket of certainty, believing we know what's what.

Meanwhile, without realizing it, that blanket turns into a barrier with the ability to separate us from the sometimes-differing perspectives and perceptions of others. It blocks us from being open to what else might be true and real. It can inhibit growth and keep us living small. This safety blanket of certainty cements us into static and toxic places of right versus wrong, creating disconnection between people and reinforcing polarization in our relationships, communities, and countries.

Our neurotic addictions to certainty have shredded relational tapestries, all because we've forgotten how to be curious. Instead, we have replaced our inquisitive openness with an egomaniacal need to prove our points, gain power, or maintain righteousness. We are afraid to leave room for the possibility someone else may also have a relevant perspective or solution. Harder yet, we hate considering the possibility we might actually be *wrong* and that ultimately, the very best thing for everyone involved (including ourselves) might be to release old beliefs, biases, and agendas that are no longer serving us and onboard something new and different.

Those fears are normal and human. So instead of throwing that safety blanket of certainty in the dumpster, let's sew in a "curiosity zipper." That way, we can unzip the blanket enough to try on what exists outside of our own experiences and perspectives while maintaining the option to retreat back into our blanket, zip it up, and choose to stick with what is familiar. We'll even make it a double-ended zipper in case you like to sleep with one foot outside the covers. This will allow you to dip your toes into varying perspectives without exposing your whole self to potentially dysregulating elements. Your willingness to use the zipper and the courage to step into actionable follow-through, when appropriate, serve as the generator powering the alignment and positive evolution of your life.

There are a few ingredients that determine whether curiosity is pure and real or not. The use of more question marks, in and of itself, is not necessarily synonymous with sincere curiosity. Asking questions according to a personal agenda, for example, can turn an inquiry into a passive-aggressive dig or a camouflaged command rather than a genuine search for truth.

For example, adults love to ask young kids, "What do you want to be when you grow up?" There seems to be a certain age threshold when answers like princess, trapeze artist, and rock star stop being acceptable. When talking to a high school student wrapping up their senior year who hasn't yet decided what to do after graduation, the question mark is sometimes saturated in the adult's personal agenda of expecting the teen should have clarity about their future career pursuits. The question becomes more of a poke in the ribs, saying to the teen, "The clock is ticking, you need to figure something out." This is the opposite of asking the question out of true curiosity without predefined expectations.

I'm not saying asking questions with an agenda can never be helpful and at times necessary. Rather, I'm encouraging an increase in our own mindful awareness around it. While having a hoped-for answer or outcome isn't necessarily a bad thing, asking questions according to an agenda doused in our own projected needs and wants has the capacity to create *disconnection*. It even has the power to cause the other person to feel self-conscious of their true answer and potentially hide it, just in case it doesn't live up to your expectations. This phenomenon of agenda'd question asking can be especially damaging when the asker lacks empathy. When being asked a question, we all want to feel able to respond in whatever way feels true to us without the risk of it being perceived as a wrong answer. Agenda is the thing that unfairly says *any* answer is wrong. When curiosity is pure, there is no such thing as a wrong answer.

Getting out of agenda is especially difficult during conflict. It takes a tremendous amount of emotional intelligence and strong self-regulation skills. If you are someone who has adamant political or religious convictions, for example, it may be quite difficult to get out of agenda when talking to someone with opposing views. If you struggle with emotional regulation, establishing connection through curiosity during conflict may feel impossible. When the priority is to prove a point or come out of the conflict as the "winner" rather than to establish true interpersonal connection, our ability to be curious gets blocked. When we are in protect-and-defend mode, the vulnerability of true curiosity is the furthest thing from comfortable. But do not underestimate the connective power of setting your own personal agenda aside for the sake of trying to understand someone else's perspective. When you ask questions during conflict, come from a sincere space of wanting to know their real answer, no matter what it is.

Bias and judgment are two more spices that, when thrown into a mixing bowl with curiosity, will ruin the recipe. Staying out of bias and judgment is, of course, much easier said than done. To anyone who says they do not carry biases (both implicit and explicit) and some level of judgment against people who think, believe, behave, and choose differently than them, I call bullshit. The human psyche is not capable of resisting bias and judgment. To say you are without either is like saying a sponge won't soak up a single drop of water when squeezed under a flowing waterfall. Owning this vulnerability within ourselves does not make us bad people. It's not personal. The sciences of psychology, neurology, and sociology show that biases and judgments are inevitable in each of us. They are part of what makes us human.

The practice of true curiosity, however, is not attached to any particular answer. It does not resist answers that are less desirable to you. It does not ask questions with the aim of fueling your next rebuttal or comeback. Curiosity in its purest form is an energy of open inquisitiveness with a completely sincere desire to better understand and learn something you didn't know prior to asking the question. This is true whether we are engaging the spirit of curiosity toward other people, within ourselves, or toward the big, giant universe that exists all around us.

You were unbridledly inquisitive when you were very young. The process of becoming more curious is one of remembering. The world has taught us to believe curiosity is risky, and certainty and righteousness equate to strength and safety. In truth, the life of the absolutist is one of fear, smallness, and (at best) lateral movement. Disconnection with oneself, other people, and the world is the result of non-curious living. It may allow you to temporarily avoid messiness, but it will keep you stuck. Dirty pain. Reject the impulse to find absolutes or stay attached to any kind of certainty. When true and sincere curiosity is your primary navigator, your human experience will be one of alignment, continuous growth, and abundant joy.

Commit to becoming more curious. And stay open.

Section 1

CONNECTION WITH YOURSELF

In my private psychotherapy practice, new clients often sit on my sofa shaking their heads and saying, "I don't understand how my life got this off track." For many of us, one or more of our train cars jumped the tracks and drove off in directions that do not line up with the stories we had written for our lives. The crazy thing is most of us can't identify when or how things got so derailed.

Aside from trauma and tragedy, dissatisfaction and stuckness don't usually happen overnight. Life misalignment is usually the result of a slow and subtle piling up of a thousand unwise decisions and unfortunate events accompanied by mindless reactivity. We don't go to bed one night with healthy teeth and wake up the next morning with a mouth full of rotted chompers. Just like we don't thrive for the first twenty-nine years of life, then show up to our thirtieth birthday party thinking, "Well damn, it's all suddenly gone to shit." This compounded breakage and blockage of our livelihood happens most often because we've spent years and years asleep at the wheel in one or more areas of our life.

There are so many ways to avoid this, starting with psychoeducation. It is not uncommon these days for kids to start learning about mindfulness in preschool or kindergarten. Teaching emotional and behavioral self-regulation tactics is much more prevalent now. When today's children, who have been educated and practiced in these things since an early age, are eventually adults, we are going to have a much more emotionally intelligent population. Psychological and mental wellness are mainstream topics now, much more so than when most of us were growing up. We are light-years beyond our parents' and grandparents' generations in our understanding and utilization of healthy psychological practices and ideas.

Fortunately for us adults who feel behind the eight ball, it's not too late to learn. The first section of this book is one big, fat lesson on how to be a more mindful, awake, aware, and psychologically well human being. You'll be guided, page by page, in exploring the inner workings of your mind, body, and heart in a way that usually only happens through transformative experiences such as psychotherapy, rehabilitation programs, and healing retreats. We're going to take a look at your biases, traumas (we all have them), dysfunctional behaviors, maladaptive beliefs, judgments, cultural and family schemas, values, and personal reactivity. You'll establish a clear understanding of what *integrity* means to you, then take inventory of how well you do or don't put your money where your mouth is through your own choices, thoughts, and behaviors.

This first section, more than any other part of the book, will require you to step out of defensiveness and justification so you can be honest about your hang-ups and strongholds. As we peel back the layers of the onion, you'll gain clarity on what needs to be reconciled, changed, or healed. You'll come out of this first section with a heightened sense of awareness. No more sleeping on the job! Welcome to your crash course on curious introspection.

Perhaps you can pinpoint a time when you stopped bulldozing long enough to lift your chin, look around, and think to yourself, "Holy shit, I've drifted way off course!" These are linchpin moments when we are called to choose between continuing with familiar monotony or challenging ourselves to step into the unknown in pursuit of something greater, something more authentic.

I remember my big linchpin moment. I was driving to work. It was seven in the morning. I had been up since 5 a.m., giving myself enough time to shower and get ready for my day, then get my daughter fed and dressed for preschool. This was a couple years before starting my career in the mental-health industry. At the time, I was clocking in and out at a job that paid the bills but brought me very little fulfillment. During my commute to work, I stopped at a red light. I reached down to loosen the buckle on my high-heeled shoe because I had strapped the right one on too tightly. I fumbled with the buckle and couldn't get the shoe off. The light was turning green, and I had a line of traffic stopped behind me. I felt the temperature of my blood increasing by the second. It had already been a long week. I was struggling with overwhelm, burnout, and high levels of stress in multiple areas of my life. I could feel an emotional breakdown coming. It's funny how something as benign as a shoe buckle can trigger such a monumental moment.

I pulled into a nearby gas station. I remember exactly where I parked my car on the north side of the lot, away from the gas pumps. I had parked in this exact same spot one month earlier, when I'd been on my drive home from work and had come down with the stomach flu. Now, I found myself looking at the same line of gas pumps while parked on top of the very spot I had barfed up shrimp cocktail all over the pavement.

Now, all in this one moment, I felt a collision of all the things that were inauthentic about my life. I hated wearing high heels. Why was I even wearing these stupid buckles to begin with? I didn't enjoy the Christian music I had been forcing myself to listen to on my morning drive every day. I hated the business clothes I was wearing. I disliked my job. I loved my husband but felt so unhappy in our marriage. The way I talked to myself in my own head felt crappy. I didn't like the way I judged other people. I avoided thinking about the future because I couldn't stand the idea it would likely be a continuation of the present.

I turned the channel on the car radio and found a station that was playing The Offspring. I cranked the volume knob all the way to the right as loud as it would play on my already-blown speakers. I grabbed the steering wheel at ten and two. And I screamed. The tears came. They streamed and streamed. The sound coming from my own throat startled me. But the discharge of all that tension felt so good, like releasing a pressure valve.

I remember feeling confused. Was I exploding into a million pieces and falling apart? Or was I cleansing all the awful, toxic, tightly wound pressure from my body? I was in agony. But getting it out felt so much better than holding it in. A vicious static had piled up too high inside me and needed emancipation. It needed to flood out through my tears. The screams were a manifestation of the pain I'd been holding inside. The sound matched what I had been feeling for far too long.

After this emotional purge, I got back on the road and made my way to work. When I arrived at my office building, I took my nylons off and threw them, along with my high-heeled shoes, in the dumpster before I walked in. I spent the entire workday wearing business-casual attire while my toes wiggled and celebrated on the floor under my cubicle desk in rebellious freedom.

That day I knew the current state and structure of my life had to end. I had no idea *how* things were going to change. I didn't even know what I wanted the *different* to look like. That cluelessness was beyond intimidating. But bigger and louder than the fears and uncertainty were the words, "*Not this*," playing on repeat in my head. I did not know a new direction for my life or how I was going to make it happen. But I was certain the way things had been could not continue.

My streaked mascara and shoeless feet tipped my department director off that something was really not okay. She pulled me aside and asked if I was all right. The tears came again. All I could do was shake my head. Our company offered Employee Assistance Program (EAP) benefits, so I got connected to our HR folks, who lovingly but boldly told me I needed to get my ass into therapy.

That day was the start of the great undoing of that former life.

It took a while. I would take some steps forward, then several steps back. I went to therapy for a while but became intimidated when faced with the significant level of change that would need to occur for me to feel better. So I eventually stopped going. I got pregnant again. I tried to convince myself this mission for life change was selfish and I should be happy and grateful for the life I already had. I purposefully turned a blind eye to the brokenness within and around me. With that avoidance mindset, it didn't take long before I became angry, resentful, and miserable again.

When I eventually accepted the need to surrender and gave up justifying all the bullshit in my life (including my own), I landed back on my previous therapist's couch. Snot ran down my face, and I sobbed as I told her there was no going back. I knew I would suffocate and become an empty shell of a human if I kept pretending I loved my life. I couldn't keep trying to convince myself everything would be okay. That dog-and-pony show was horse shit, and I knew it.

During past appointments, my therapist had patiently allowed me to hijack every session with verbal vomit of all the things I was unhappy with. The purging catharsis had been necessary. But now, it was time to get down to business and do the actual *work*.

My therapist stopped allowing me to spend the entirety of our sessions venting. Instead, she challenged me to look inward. She would ask me, "What do you notice in your body?" when I described distressing situations. She'd stop me, midsentence sometimes, and encourage me to quit talking for a minute. She would prompt me, "Feel whatever it is you are feeling." "If there is sadness," she'd say, "feel that fully." She taught me that talking about my feelings was only one little part of therapeutic processing and on its own wasn't enough. I had to *feel* it all and move *through* the pain, not just talk about it.

Accountability became a weekly norm. My therapist would make me identify one thing I felt shitty about in my life, then she'd throw down a goal to create a small shift or change before our next session. She especially encouraged me to make *internal* change a priority.

My thoughts were the first internal thing she addressed. I began to recognize they were full of negativity, anger, and judgment (toward myself and others). These thoughts almost completely ran the show. Like any good mental-health clinician, my therapist would call me on my bullshit when I made excuses for my doom-and-gloom mentalities. She taught me first how to identify scarcity-based thoughts, then eventually how to reframe, reroute, and transform them.

Curious introspection wasn't totally new to me. But inner accountability was. I'd never realized I had this much power over the climate of my inner experience. The way I thought and felt was *my* responsibility, no one else's. This was a major epiphany!

I learned to be patient and curious with myself. I learned the value of self-care and self-compassion. These were things I had always believed to be "selfish," a message that had been planted and reinforced by my chronic and generationally inherited codependency, my Lutheran upbringing, and every influential person who had ever told me I need to be self-sacrificing and holistically other-person focused.

Now I was learning, for the first time in my life, that questioning things isn't bad. Speaking up when something feels shitty would not make me sprout devil horns or turn me into a terrible person. This new courage and curiosity pissed some people off, for sure. But it empowered me. It helped me, little by little, to begin remembering who I was.

Real, authentic, and aligned life evolution does not start with external change. It does not begin with a situational shift or other people changing in ways that would make you feel better. It starts first by going inward and making observations. It continues with the willingness to practice true, non-agenda'd curiosity *within yourself*. When you break a bone, the healing process doesn't start by throwing a cast on it. First, you notice the pain. You feel it. You communicate to others that you might need help. Then, you take x-rays to learn more. You douse the pain with curiosity so you can gather information about the injury itself. Finally, you decide on a treatment. The casting perhaps comes in its own good and appropriate time. Healing requires patience, care, and consistency. Eventually the cast comes off, and you learn to use the limb again. Sometimes you have to take steps backward to regain strength that has been lost. If you trust the process and do so with intention, conviction, and tenacity, you come out the other side prepared to get back to the business of living life in a way that is much more impactful and fulfilling than what was ever going to be possible with the un-tended-to injury.

You can't skip steps. You have to start at the beginning. It is sometimes the scariest part.

We go within.

With the general rise in emotional and psychological awareness in recent years, "mindfulness" has become quite the buzzword. With its origins in ancient eastern and Buddhist philosophies, the concept of mindfulness dates back a couple thousand years. But it didn't really hit our culturally familiar scene until the late twentieth century.

Mindfulness

We are, by nature, mindful beings. When we learn about our five senses in preschool or kindergarten, it isn't new information to us. Those lessons are just giving us a more explicit understanding of and language to describe the felt experiences we've been having since before we were even born. The sense of hearing, for example, kicks in for an unborn baby around the eighteenth week of pregnancy. That's about the time when we begin to hear our mother's heartbeat and digestive noises. And even though it takes some time for our other senses, like clear sight and a full range of taste, to develop, we implicitly notice a large range of sensory experiences long before we are given words for them.

When is the last time you laid still and paid attention to something as simple as the sound of a heartbeat? Or closed your eyes so you could turn your noticing energy toward the amazing smell of something sweet baking in the oven or the feeling of a warm, tight hug from someone you love? When did you last take off your shoes and socks to feel blades of grass between your toes? Or sit on a park bench and pay attention to nothing other than the changing formations of a group of ducks swimming across a pond?

Mindfulness requires us to disengage from the busy chaos of life to gently notice things in and around us. It is the most docile and subtle form of curiosity. True mindfulness lacks judgment and agenda. It involves a tender acknowledgment of a thing with zero desire or intention to change it, understand it, stop it, or do something about, to, or with it. Mindfulness also lacks the need or desire to make the thing continue. The spirit of mindfulness is one that understands change is inevitable. Because of that, holding onto, changing, or pushing away the thing we are noticing is unnecessary. The desire to do any of those things takes away your ability to simply be present in the noticing. Present in the moment.

When I was a kid, one of my favorite things to do was lie on my back in the grass and watch the clouds as they changed shape and moved across the sky. During an activity like that, there's no control to be had over the speed the clouds travelled. There's no judgment to pass on the shape or size of one cloud compared to the next. Nature is full of miracles like that. Little reminders that Mother Nature is ultimately the one in control, not us. She was here long before you, and she'll be here long after. When you want to enhance your mindfulness practice, nature is a great place to do it.

Fall is my favorite time of year in Colorado. Toward the end of September, the aspen trees turn to shades like flames. One fall weekend per year, Coloradoans swarm the mountain roads to catch a peek at the aspen leaves changing from green to yellow to orange to red. This special color-change weekend is one of the reasons I may never move away from Colorado. I love it that much.

A few years ago, I was swamped with work throughout the month of September. I was hired for a multi-day speaking gig on the east coast, then traveled straight to the Midwest for another presentation. I returned home to Denver on a Sunday after a seven-day stint of business travel. I jumped straight into a full docket of clients at my private practice the next morning. I crammed in snacks and pee breaks wherever I could, returned phone calls during my commutes to and from the office and in between sessions, and left my suitcase packed with dirty clothes in the corner of the bedroom. At the end of each night, I collapsed into bed, hoping to get at least six hours of sleep before waking up to start the sprint all over again the next morning.

By Monday night the week I returned from traveling, I felt exhausted. By Tuesday night, I was grouchy and wanted my family to leave me alone. By Wednesday night, I was in tears, miserable, and trying to rationalize quitting my job, closing my practice, and going to work at the local Starbucks. On Thursday, I almost cried tears of joy when my noon client had to cancel at the last minute. Wisdom from somewhere deep within me knew better than to try and crank out some administrative work or squeeze in a quick workout during this unexpected break in my day. Rather, I needed to be still. My whole system was craving it.

I lit a candle and dropped my ass onto the big, comfy sofa where my clients sit during their sessions. I sat on the edge of the cushion with my large office windows behind me. I planted both feet on the ground, closed my eyes, dropped my shoulders out of my ears (which they had decided was their default position over the past couple weeks), and took a few deep breaths. Silent tears immediately wet my face. A breakdown would ruin my productivity for the rest of the day, my "hold your shit together" mentality, and my mascara. I didn't have the time or space for a full-blown crash. So instead, I breathed, inhales and exhales, for a long time. I used the five-four-three-two-one mindfulness grounding exercise I teach clients. I sat and noticed:

- ✓ five things I could see (lights, colors, spacing between things, shapes, smudges on the floorboards)

- ✓ four things I could feel (firmness of the ground, softness of the blanket, coolness of the air conditioning, a part of my ponytail that was pulled a little too tight)

- ✓ three things I could hear (my white-noise machine, the muffled sounds of someone talking in my lobby, cars on the street outside three floors below)

- ✓ two things I could smell (the lavender oil running in my diffuser, my suitemate's microwaved lunch)

✓ one thing I could taste (remnants of a protein bar I had scarfed down before my last session that were still stuck in my teeth)

I didn't move when I finished the grounding routine. The stillness felt too dang good. I was afraid if I opened my eyes, the chaos and overwhelm would be hovering over me, waiting to gobble me up again. I just sat.

Inhale.

Exhale.

I let my thoughts peck away at me, like the minnows that eat dead skin off people's feet during those weird fish pedicures. I didn't try to kick the thoughts away. My breath and my five senses were keeping me safe and connected to the earth. I knew the pecking thoughts couldn't hurt me. I simply allowed them to be there but refrained from giving them the power of my attention.

After some time, I needed to "wake up" and get ready for my 1 p.m. client. I wiggled my fingers and toes, then blinked my eyes open to a brighter-than-I-remembered room. As I stood up and turned around to fluff the sofa pillows, something outside stopped me in my tracks. The window of my office was not subtle. It covered the entire twelve-foot wall. Outside the window was a small grove of aspen trees. This was my fourth day back in town and in the office seeing clients in that exact same room, with that exact same window looking out at those exact same aspens. But for the first time all week, I noticed thousands of fluttering, neon-yellow aspen leaves.

When I had left town two weeks prior, the leaves had all been green with no hint of the fall change. This brilliant sight took my breath away. It felt like a punch in the stomach. In another day or two, the leaves would be orange and red. I had almost missed yellow entirely. I had been here since Monday and not even noticed the gigantic, changing trees right outside my window. The sight was shocking. How was it possible I had missed this thing? It had been right in front of my face all week.

Then, a second sock to the gut. If I had missed this, what else had slipped through the cracks? I had seen my kids each night after work, but I had no idea how their days at school had been or their moods were. I was oblivious to all the work my husband had done to keep the home ship afloat while I had been away. I couldn't even remember whether or not I had pet my dog since I'd returned home on Sunday night.

I won't soon forget that experience. Mother Nature smacked me in the face with exactly the thing she knew would get my attention. She reminded me what happens when I bulldoze through my days. Since then, whenever I don't feel quite like myself, I know to slow down, breathe, and dial back into a mindful state of being. When I can find stillness inside myself, I engage with the world around me in a more awake and aware way. I'm so much more present.

The concept of mindfulness is central to a life of flow, presence, and alignment. Without mindfulness, it is *impossible* to intimately know or feel like yourself. Without mindfulness, we miss out on the subtleties of the human experience, which are often the best parts.

Up your mindfulness game. Practice it. Exercise it. There are bazillions of apps, articles, books, documentaries, facilities, and professionals out there to use as resources. If it is an unfamiliar concept to you, do a quick search on Google or Pinterest and grow to understand it more. Integrate intentional mindfulness practices into your daily life. It is simple, free, and significantly life giving.

Mindfulness, more so than any other one thing you will learn in this book, will dial you directly back into your humanity. It will inform, teach, and guide you. In your pursuit of authenticity and alignment, you will return to mindfulness again and again and again. It will become your anchor and your compass, grounding you and leading you back to yourself.

A sub-category of mindfulness is introspection. It is one of the most important components of self-actualization. Introspection is the turning of your observational energy away from the incessant static of external stimulation back toward what is happening *inside* you. It's like driving in one direction in your car, then flipping a U-turn. Introspection is a learnable,

U-turns + Three Buckets

practicable skill that, when exercised consistently, creates a harmonious, dual-directional balance for your most valuable commodity—your attention.

It's easy to get mindlessly lost amid the infinite external competition for our attention. The world around us provides a constant barrage of stimuli, each (whether naturally or purposefully) fighting for its place in the forefronts of our minds. People want our time, opinions, and help.

Pets want us to scratch behind their ears. Employers expect us to give of our skills and energy. Our romantic partners want their feet rubbed, anniversaries remembered, and for us to make out with them. Our children expect us to feed them meals and tuck them into bed at night. Ugh, and don't get me started on the media's incessant pull on our time and attention. News articles and campaigns are in our faces, begging for us to read and watch them. The infrastructure of social media platforms is designed to lure us in, capture our attention, and keep us sucked into the bottomless black hole of infinite scrolling. There are beautiful mountains to hike, fabulous streaming TV shows to binge, beaches to play on, and museums to explore. There are KU college basketball games to watch, worries to ruminate on, weather to check, vacations to plan, bills to pay, difficult interactions to predict and prevent, workouts to fit in, emails to return, lunches to pack, chiropractor appointments to schedule, speeding tickets to pay, things to order from Amazon...the list of things lobbying for our consideration, emotional and physical energy, time, and resources is legitimately never-ending!

This relentless demand for our attention yanks both our conscious and subconscious energies toward things outside of us. Do you ever pause from that rat race to look inward? For just a moment, allow yourself to be curious about the time and energy you spend intentionally U-turning your attention toward what is happening *inside* yourself. It is not uncommon for my brand-new therapy clients to say, "I never do that, and I'm not totally sure I even know what you are talking about." If that's you, don't worry. We'll turn you into an introspective, U-turning pro in no time.

Our inner experiences run a constant ticker tape of wisdom in an attempt to help and inform us. Without introspection, we are without a compass. We spend most of our focus on the road ahead of us, putting one foot in front of the other, pursuing a life of onward and upward movement. That's all good and necessary. But when your eyes are only on the road ahead, you set yourself up for a life full of blind spots and misalignments. Nothing will make you feel less like yourself than mindlessly wandering away from your innermost guidance. Introspection brings us back home, into ourselves.

I've heard it said that people fall into two general categories: those who refill their car's gas tank when it has dropped below half-full, and those who wait until the tank is damn near empty. I'm in the cohort of risk-takers, living on the edge, tempting the universe to leave me stranded on the side of the highway, two hundred yards from the exit with the next gas station. The way I figure it, I'm minimizing the cumulative number of minutes I spend at gas stations throughout my life. It's a matter of efficiency.

Here's the problem with the way I do it. I have a bad habit of not paying attention to the warning lights in my car. So my gas light may be glowing bright orange and the screen is telling me I have five miles to empty, but I don't know it because I forget to pay attention. My check-engine light could be lit up, accompanied by a grinding noise coming from the undercarriage, but I'm oblivious because my focus is holistically elsewhere. My lack of mindful attention to my car's needs has left me stranded on the side of the road an embarrassing number of times. My car once ran out of gas in the middle of a busy intersection during a torrential downpour. My mindless negligence has made me late and caused inconvenient detours. I made it through my entire freshman year of college without changing the oil in my four-door, rusted, brown Ford Taurus (her name was Delores) simply because I never paid attention to the warning signals or maintenance schedule. The engine exploded. Lesson learned.

When we are introspectively negligent, we increase the probability of unnecessary struggle, aggravation, stress, and burnout. In my private practice, therapeutic progress is dead in the water unless a client is able to establish and utilize mindful introspection skills. It is impossible to create healing or meaningful change (much less a sustained post-therapy level of wellness) when a person overidentifies with their *external* life circumstances or triggers. I teach clients how to use this concept of U-turns to observe what's happening *inside* themselves regularly throughout the day. They learn to pay attention to the warning lights and insights that come to them through their thoughts, feelings, and physical sensations.

Try this exercise. Imagine there are three orange Home Depot buckets on the floor in front of you mostly filled with water. In each bucket, there are various ephemera settled on the bottom: leaves, glitter, bugs, flower petals, sand, scraps of paper—whatever comes to mind.

Imagine you take a stick and stir one of those buckets up. You notice the debris get caught up in the movement of the water. They change position, swirl around, perhaps rise to the top, right? Now imagine you take the stick out. After a few moments, the swirl of the water and movement of the floating stuff starts to slow. The solids eventually drift to a settled stop on the bottom of the bucket. With even more time, the surface of the water becomes still again. Close your eyes and spend at least sixty seconds observing this visualization.

Nicely done. And congratulations, you just totally meditated! Now let's make some sense of this mind trick. Remember that there are actually three buckets. The differentiation of each bucket is one of the most important components of introspection.

Bucket #1: Cognitions

Of all three buckets, the contents of this first one tend to be the easiest to assign words to. In this cognitive bucket, the floating elements have messages on them. They might be scraps of paper or text bubbles. The collection of these floating pieces represents our internal cognitive experience.

The word "cognitive" refers to *things of the mind*. It includes everything from your thoughts, judgments, and wonderings to your inner banter and the conversations you have with yourself. Cognitions are the worries that keep you awake in the middle of the night and the words you replay in your head, over and over again, after a hard conversation. They include your daydreams, the lyrics to the song stuck in your head, the plans you are making for tomorrow's grocery-store trip, and the fears you have about the future. Learning, visualization, and memorization are highly cognitive activities. So are the listening and attention aspects of engaging with other people. Your cognitive experience runs constantly, especially during your waking hours; although your cognitive engine runs somewhat during your sleep and dream states too.

I found the most usable description of what happens in the cognitive bucket in the book *The Untethered Soul* by Michael Singer. Singer refers to our constant stream of cognitions as the voice of our inner roommate. "Basically, you are not alone in there," he writes. Using your Home Depot bucket visualization tool, imagine everything your inner roommate says is represented by a floating element in your bucket.

After reading Singer's book, I started to step back and consider what kind of a roomie situation I had going on in my own head. My first observation was that my inner roommate never shuts up. Good grief, she talks a lot! Sometimes, I want to finish my workday, sit on my porch swing with my dogs, and quietly relax while I watch the sunset. But my roommate follows me everywhere I go and talks, talks, talks, talks, talks. She knows I have a lot to do, and she wants things done the right way, right now. She sees the improvements that need to happen in every plan, the holes in every argument, the to-do list that needs constant attention. My cognitive bucket is usually packed to the gills with scraps of paper and text bubbles full of all the things my inner roommate is saying.

My cognitive roommate has a really hard time sitting still. Sometimes she'll wake me up in the middle of the night to remind me of the phone calls I need to make in the morning. She'll yack at me about the conversation I need to have with a business colleague, the shopping list I need to put together, and the specific clothing items I need to pack for a quick weekend trip

I'm leaving for in another six days. She is relentless! When I wake up in the morning, step into the shower, and look down at my belly, my roommate says to me, "Hey, girl, you really could have done without that ice cream last night." Ugh, she can be such a critical asshole sometimes. My roommate is always holding my to-do list over my head. She follows me around with a clipboard of items that she wants me to complete. The floating elements in my own cognitive-bucket visualization often include Post-it notes galore, each with a reminder of things I need to take care of written on it:

- ✓ schedule a haircut

- ✓ register kids for golf lessons

- ✓ return books to the library

- ✓ fold laundry

- ✓ get phone screen repaired

- ✓ plan for husband's birthday

- ✓ return voice messages

- ✓ shave legs

- ✓ research better running shoes

- ✓ schedule oil change for the car

- ✓ text girlfriends to plan coffee date

✓ find an organization to volunteer for

✓ pick up dog food

✓ pick up dog poop

✓ refinance the house

✓ get a workout in

✓ floss teeth

✓ replace pillowcases

✓ wash car

And so on, forever and ever until the end of time.

Sometimes I want to punch my cognitive roommate in her stupid face, break her clipboard, and set every single one of her sticky-note reminders on fire. Once, while hiking to the summit of a 14er in the Rocky Mountains, out of breath, exhausted, and surrounded by beauty, my inner roommate was trying to outline the introduction of a speaking gig I had coming up three weeks later. How annoying!

When I first read Singer's *The Untethered Soul,* I was (for the first time ever in my life) confronted with the notion that me and my thoughts are not one and the same. There are multiple aspects of my inner being. Singer explains, "The first is you, the awareness, the witness, the center of your willful intentions; and the other is that which you watch." We are separate. My chatterbox cognitive roommate is one thing. I am another. I am the witnesser of my roommate. I am the observer of my thoughts. I can look down into my cognitive bucket and see each of the messages my inner roommate provides. My thoughts are not *me*.

The realization that my *thoughts are just thoughts* was a huge epiphany. My cognitions don't determine or define what's real. My inner roommate is convinced she's a time traveler who has the ability to change the past or determine the future. She's neurotic like that. In reality, most of the things my inner roommate worries about never end up happening at all.

Consider that your own inner roommate's chatter is represented by the objects and words that float around in your first Home Depot bucket. Begin to pay attention to what you see when you look down into that bucket. Notice what kinds of things your inner roommate spends thought-based energy on. What parts of the day does she tend to chatter more? Does your roommate wake up slowly in the morning and ease into the day, the water and floating elements in the bucket shifting with gentle movement? Or does she bombard you as soon as your alarm goes off, sending everything in the bucket into a miniature hurricane? Do the contents of this bucket get louder and faster when you are in an argument with someone? When life slows down and gets a little still, does your roommate get calm? Or does she become antsy and speak up more?

At any given moment, it is important to be able to step back and witness your inner roommate's banter, as she reminds you of the contents of your cognitive bucket. Your roommate's energy will match the speed and intensity at which the contents of your bucket swirl. Notice your own Home Depot bucket of cognitions on the floor in front of you. Do you often get caught up in believing you are *in* the bucket, trying to tread water as you swim among all the thoughts, all the words? It can be tricky to remember that, in reality, you are on the outside, the *observer* looking down into the bucket. Mindful awareness of your cognitions requires you to consciously step *out* of the bucket, take a few steps back, and look down into it with curiosity.

This is *cognitive introspection*. It is a gentle noticing of what's happening in your mind at any given time. Practice this exercise of looking down and observing the contents, movement, and speed of whatever is floating around in this first bucket. Experiment with it when you are calm, then again at another time, perhaps when you are in the midst of stress or adversity. See how the temperament of your inner roommate and the contents of your cognitive bucket shift and change, speed up or slow down when you are in a good mood versus when you are having a tough day. There is no judgment to be had about whatever you notice. Rather, this mindful cognitive introspection is a practice of sincere curiosity toward the bustle of your mind. As you observe, try to stay in a non-agenda'd mindset, with no more emotional charge than the sentiment, "Isn't that interesting?"

Bucket #2: Emotions

The second Home Depot bucket houses our *emotional experiences*. These may work in conjunction with the cognitions that swim around in our first bucket, but they are not the same. When we look down into this second bucket, we don't see thoughts or words. And there's no inner roommate giving us the play-by-play, sideline report of this bucket. Instead, the elements floating around in this bucket are *emotional sensations,* notable occurrences of the heart.

These are harder to put words to because they are *felt* experiences. For the sake of this visualization exercise, consider your emotions in whatever forms feel true to you. Anger, for example, might be a red-hot branding iron or a fire-engine siren. Sadness might show up as a gloomy, gray rain cloud. Excitement might be depicted by a fast-swimming silver minnow that darts through the water in the bucket. Try really hard not to get overly logical about the contents of this second bucket. Let your imagination show you what feels accurate. Emotions, after all, are not about logic. They are about feelings.

The emotional elements moving around in this second bucket may be calm and settled, or they may be swirling and mixing together. We may notice one easily identifiable emotion moving around in this second bucket, or a dozen different emotions that may or may not even make rational sense to us.

I feel silly saying this, but when I learned emotions are different and separate from thoughts, it was new news to me. Prior to that, when someone asked how I *felt* about something, I defaulted to telling them what I *thought* about it. If they asked, "How did you *feel* about the Black Widow plot twist in the *Avengers: End Game* movie?" I would answer with, "I *think* it was a smart choice and a creative plot swerve." However, the appropriate answer to that particular question would have been, "I first felt confused, then scared, then totally devastated!" When asked a bucket-*one*-related question, be sure to answer with a cognitive observation. When asked a bucket-*two*-related question, don't give a cognition-based answer. Rather, step back and observe what *emotions* you are *feeling* and provide an answer that best represents that emotionally felt sensation.

Curiosity toward our second-bucket contents, our *emotions,* utilizes and strengthens emotional intelligence. For many people, the older we get, the more we desensitize our intuitive connection to our feelings in the service of cognitive analysis. We prefer to seek safety and certainty in the perceived *under-standing* of something rather than simply allowing ourselves to notice and *feel* our feelings.

Remember the emotions chart that hangs in kindergarten classrooms? Under each expressive emoji face is the name of the corresponding emotion. Of course, the obvious emotions are feelings like happy, sad, angry, confused, and excited. As adults, our vocabulary for this collection of internal experiences is much more robust than that of the six-year-olds in the kinder-garten class. So make sure to consider emoji faces for complex emotions such as disappointed, worried, overwhelmed, intim-idated, and apprehensive. Don't forget the more pleasant side of the emotional range, including eager, twitterpated, relaxed, awed, and joyful.

Be cautious not to fall into the trap of misidentifying one emotion as another, especially when various feelings have a common thread or a similar internal expression. Uncomfort-able is not the same feeling as irritated. Happy is not the same feeling as excited. Anger and rage are related but ultimately different feelings. Emotional intelligence skyrockets when we develop the ability to differentiate between emotions, especially those that can be interpreted similarly if we haven't worked to become mindfully aware enough to feel the difference. The ability to specifically and precisely identify feelings without misinterpreting them is called *emotional granularity*.

High levels of emotional granularity and awareness are exhibited by individuals who report consistently and sustainably feeling *like themselves*. Conversely, people who report feeling lost, stuck, and disconnected from their true selves tend to struggle to identify and non-judgmentally embrace the contents of this second Home Depot bucket. Challenge yourself to notice your emotions on a more observant level. Make it a practice to differentiate between your varying emotions.

We tend to resist embracing difficult emotions. We avoid, numb, overmedicate, distract from, and deflect emotions that don't feel good. A sentiment in *Untamed* by Glennon Doyle caught my attention. She writes about a monumental moment when she learned the value of identifying and honoring her bucket-two emotional contents. Glennon writes, "Feeling all your feelings is hard, but that's what they're for. Feelings are for feeling."

If authentically and wholeheartedly feeling our feelings is the whole reason they exist, and if doing so provides value, then perhaps it is true there are *no bad feelings*. There are certainly emotional experiences that are less fun than others. I, for one, would much rather spend an hour feeling hopeful than spend an hour in terror, for instance. Even so, emotions are no more deserving of judgment than something like the color yellow. I've got too much of an olive complexion to look good in yellow clothing, and I wouldn't paint my house the same color as the highlighter pen I use to mark up my books. But the color yellow itself is neither good nor bad. It's just a color. It's not right nor wrong. Maybe your very favorite color is yellow. Not me; I prefer blue or gray. That doesn't make either of us right or wrong.

When it comes to emotions, isn't it interesting how much judgment we all have against the less comfortable ones? This bias against certain feelings starts early. I'm as guilty as the next person of judging emotions, particularly when they cause my kids to be especially irrational. When my son was little and got upset that another kid at daycare snatched up his Hot Wheels truck, and when he felt so frustrated and sad that tears rolled down his cheeks, it was tempting to roll my eyes and tell him to "get over it." Ugh, how often do we do this to our kids?! From our adult perspective, this situation seems too petty for tears. So our tolerance goes out the window. We silly adults have forgotten that rationality is not a fair or appropriate measure of emotion. Logic and reason are the currencies of cognitions, not emotions. It doesn't work to use words and logic to explain the experience of rage, for example, to someone who has never experienced that feeling. At least, not in a way that will allow them to truly *know* what it feels like to have the specific experience of rage inside them.

Just like bucket one, the contents of bucket two are data. Regardless of whether they are fluffy, cozy, and soothing or spikey, sharp, and burdensome, all emotions show up packed full of information. They tell us when one thing feels good and another feels icky. They help us identify what kind of environments we want or don't want to be in, what kinds of relationships feel the best to us, and what types of art we feel drawn to. They indicate whether we prefer classical music or (in my case) rocking out to 1990s grunge and alternative. Our feelings alert us when we've done something wrong. They put us on guard when there is risk of danger. They remind us of experiences from the past when they get triggered by something in the here and now. *All* emotions are important. Not just the pleasant ones.

One of the most common obstacles new psychotherapy clients must overcome when they step into my private practice is their aversion to feeling hard emotions. Many people don't mind *talking* about them, but they rarely want to *feel* them. An especially skeptical woman once asked me, "Why would I voluntarily chose to step into an appointment every week when I know I will likely cry and have to feel hard feelings?" "Because," I told her, "you are not half-human. It is impossible to opt out of half your emotions without suffering consequences from that avoidance." Your attempt to dodge hard emotions will ultimately lead to a watered-down human experience. That is not an authentic way to live. You will never feel whole-heartedly *like yourself* as long as you dismiss, deflect, or avoid uncomfortable feelings.

When we embrace and honor that all feelings are for *feeling* and we don't need to be afraid of them, the world opens up for infinite growth, change, and possibility. It enables us to realize we can handle tough feelings and in fact learn profound things from the most emotionally painful experiences. If you've ever felt the sting of tremendous loss and the suffocating weight of grief, you know what it feels like to be fully human. Grief specifically has a way of reminding us we aren't robots. The same goes for anger, fear, and all the other uncomfortable emotions. Isn't it so interesting that joy, excitement, and satisfaction remind us of that same humanness? They are just on the other end of the emotional spectrum.

Your ability to live a life authentically *as yourself* is contingent on your willingness to increase and improve your emotional intelligence game by observing and courageously embracing *all* the feels, not just the pleasant ones. In any given moment, you can be mindfully curious about your feelings by stepping outside of your emotions bucket and peering down at its contents. When you peek into your bucket, notice the angry fireballs, the gently floating feathers of comfort and coziness, the turtle hiding in his shell out of embarrassment. Don't worry if you feel multiple opposing feelings at the same time. That may feel confusing, but it is totally normal. Stay out of judgment. Simply observe and fully *feel*. Your emotional bucket has wisdom to offer you, humanity to remind you of, and empathy to equip you with.

Bucket #3: Somatics

The word "somatic" means "of the body." It refers to felt physical experiences. Of the three buckets, this is the trickiest one for many people to connect with. For them, looking down into the somatic bucket and observing the contents feels confusing and even inaccessible. For other individuals, somatics are the obvious, primary, and most pronounced internal messengers of them all. I often see a strong connection of mindful awareness to this third bucket in people who do body work or physical labor for a living: dancers, massage therapists, construction workers, artists, athletes, and yoga instructors.

When we move aside the cognitive and emotional buckets, what remains is an enormous repertoire of information that is constantly broadcast to us in the form of physical sensations throughout our bodies. As you look down into this third Home Depot bucket, these somatic elements are the things you *physically and energetically feel* when you take a head-to-toe inventory of what's happening in your body.

Like the emotions bucket, what you notice in your somatic bucket won't always make logical or rational sense. For example, you might be familiar with the sensation of "butterflies in your stomach" when stepping on a stage for a performance, going on a first date, or sitting down for an important interview. There obviously isn't a flock of monarchs fluttering around in your guts. Rather, that's the best way we can explain the physical sensation we sometimes feel when we are nervous or excited. Depressive heaviness in your torso may feel like an elephant standing on your chest. Tightness in your throat when you are trying not to cry is sometimes described as swallowing a golf ball. When I experience anxiety, I sometimes look down into my somatic bucket and notice a physical feeling of jittery electricity, as if my body is plugged into an electrical socket.

Some of these data come to us through our five senses: sight, taste, touch, smell, and sound. Checking what's happening throughout our five senses is a great way to curiously peek down into our somatic bucket. On the day I realized all the aspen leaves had turned yellow, I used the five-four-three-two-one mindfulness exercise to get there. This exercise is useful in helping us become more observant of the contents of our third bucket. We know it may not be safe to approach a dog when our sense of hearing informs us the animal's bark or growl is aggressive. The feeling of hot cement in the summertime might activate, through our sense of touch, the response of hopping off the sidewalk and into the grass before we scorch the bottoms of our feet. A trigger (the dog's bark or the hot cement in these examples) serves as the bucket's stirring stick. Triggers swirl the contents in our somatic bucket, disrupting the calm of our physical bodies with noticeable sensations.

If you pay close attention, you'll notice you are in a constant state of somatic experience. Some somatics are acute or disturbing. Others are subtle or benign. Sharp, stabbing pain when you step on a Lego with a bare foot is an obvious and startling somatic sensation. But keep in mind, a feeling of relaxation throughout your body is a no-less-important piece of data, even though it involves no pain or threat of injury. The sound of the air conditioning kicking on, the sudden brightness of the morning sun when you throw open the bedroom curtains, and the warmth on the palm of your hand when it's placed on your kid's forehead to see if they might have a fever—all are information-communicating elements of your somatic network. A growling stomach or shaky hands might be a reminder you need to eat. A racing heart rate may be a piece of information telling you that something feels unsafe. Your job is to observe, identify, and be curious about what you notice in this bucket, trusting that these physical experiences carry wisdom that deserves attention.

The correlation and connection between our psychological and physical experiences are called "psychosomatics." When I experience stress, the muscles in my shoulders and neck bunch up into knots. One time, years ago, I got off a super-intense phone call and found I couldn't turn my head. The muscles in my neck and shoulders had seized up. I hadn't slept on them wrong, and I hadn't strained anything during a workout. The tension, pain, and loss of mobility were direct results of the escalated phone interaction and the stress I was experiencing because of it. My body *knew*! Psychosomatic distress can often be misinterpreted as a medical issue. Of course, when your body talks to you, there might be a biological or medical reason for what you are physically feeling. But it is also possible your physical body is trying to shine some light on something occurring on a psychological level.

Get to know your common somatic responses as they relate to the various relationships, environments, moods, and situations in your life. When I'm working hard or deep in concentration, I clench my jaw. I notice a general physical contraction or relaxation depending on which people I'm around. Certain environments evoke very specific physical reactions within me. My body feels one way when I'm sitting at my office desk for the eighth consecutive hour working on a business project. An entirely different barrage of physical experiences exists when I'm lying on a beach by the ocean or snuggled up with my husband and kids watching a movie on our sofa at home. The weather can even sometimes be a contributor to sensations I feel throughout my body. I tend to feel much higher levels of energy and bounciness on warm, spring days. On gloomy, cold-weather days, I'm much more likely to be dragging ass and feeling tiredness and fatigue throughout my whole body. The physical body is such an incredible barometer for what's happening in and around us.

The somatic bucket can sometimes be hard to observe, especially for highly cognitive individuals. One of my clients, for example, works as a specialist in the aerospace-technology industry. Her thinking abilities are her superpower—this woman is brilliant. The first time she told me about a hard experience from her life, she was able to easily articulate her *thoughts* about it. She also had decent access to some of the *emotions* it caused her to feel. But when I asked what this memory evoked *in her body*, she looked at me like I had three heads and was speaking a foreign language. She said, "Can you ask that in a different way?" "Sure," I said and changed my wording. "As you allow that memory to come up, what physical sensations do you notice in your body?" The client still looked confused and responded with an answer that told me she was going to need some somatic-mindfulness training. I'm happy to report that now, after intentional and consistent mindfulness training and practice, this client is one of the most equipped people I know when it comes to listening to what her body is trying to communicate. But isn't it interesting how disconnected from her body she was at first? This is common, especially for those of us who rely heavily on our analytical abilities much of the time. Difficulty observing the somatic bucket's contents is also common in individuals who have experienced physical trauma or sexual abuse. Disconnection from their own bodies has become a protective mechanism for some of these folks.

Schools are getting much better at educating children on how to connect with their somatic expressions. We equip kids with so much power when we help them learn to detect, observe, and communicate their physical sensations. When a child speaks up about an emotion or worry he has, a great follow-up question is, "Where do you feel that in your body?" If five-year-old Suzie says she's feeling frustrated, for example, she might say she notices she's clenching her fists or wants to stomp her feet. When young Alex says he feels nervous before his dentist appointment, he might say it feels like grasshoppers are bouncing around in his stomach.

This work is no less important for grownups. A meaningful connection to our physical sensations helps us return to the inherent mindful attunement that has often become blunted by the time we reach adulthood. The ability to step back and observe what's happening in your somatic bucket is a gift that will increase your level of mindfulness in a way no amount of thinking or emoting can achieve. Make it a practice and a discipline.

Overall, understanding the concept of the three buckets and establishing the ability to notice their contents will help you receive the clues and guidance your system wants to provide you. The next time you feel triggered, overwhelmed, or generally not like yourself, practice identifying the contents of your three buckets: your thoughts, your emotions, and your physical sensations. Getting curious enough to nonjudgmentally observe the contents of the buckets will help you separate yourself from your internal experiences, reminding you that you are not your thoughts. You are not your emotions. You are not your physical sensations. You are *you*, the witness of these things.

Learn to identify when you have become lost *in* the bucket. Then teach yourself how to get *out* of it. Getting out, by the way, does not mean getting rid of the experiences. Rather, it means learning to recognize you are the *observer* of the experiences. That separation helps. By learning to unblend from your internal experiences, you can feel more like *yourself,* even while experiencing the contents of your three buckets. When you feel overwhelmed, as though you are drowning in the swirling flotsam of your buckets, parse it all out into the three separate categories. Simplify what feels complex.

With these, your very own three Home Depot buckets, you have a new tool. Never again do you have to feel lost amid the sometimes-chaotic thoughts, emotions, and physical sensations in your mind, heart, and body.

Every single one of us has mental health issues. Read that again. Mental wellness, which is more appropriately called "psychological wellness" since it involves so much more than just our mental states, is a spectrum. We all fluctuate through varying levels of psychological okayness throughout our lives. Hell, sometimes mine changes multiple times in a day! There

States of Arousal

is no dividing line between those who have mental health issues and those who don't. Rather, it's a matter of where you land on the spectrum in any given moment, situation, or phase of life. This stuff is, truly, an unavoidable part of being human.

Considering that altered psychological states have a tremendous capacity to block us from feeling like ourselves, it's important we work to understand them better. One big, fat nontruth I'd like to blow out of the water is that mental health struggles are primarily rooted in an inability to regulate emotions. The truth is dysregulated emotions are a byproduct, a side effect, of something that often starts from a much more scientific and empirically observable place. We tend to blame our crappy feelings on someone or something else or chalk them up to our own inadequacies and inability to handle life. When you don't feel like yourself and have trouble functioning at a psychologically healthy and optimized level, come back to the science and find relief in remembering *you are not crazy.*

When we see adverse mental health symptoms, many people still automatically point to "chemical imbalances in the brain." Chemical contributors certainly play a role in a person's psychological functioning. But failing to recognize the influence of the electrical energy coursing throughout the brain and body is like taking your car with a dead battery to the repair shop and only having them change the oil and fill the gas tank. If the battery is short circuiting, there's no amount of coolant that can be topped off to make that car run properly. Your body is like a car in the sense that there is a correlation between the electricity and the chemistry. If the electricity is imbalanced, no amount of chemical correction on its own will result in healing, relief, or positive change.

The human brain has a tremendous amount of energy surging through it. The varying electrical wavelengths running throughout our brains contribute to everything we experience, from how fast we fall asleep or how well we focus, to how successfully we hold our shit together when something upsets us. Unbalanced electrical energy in the brain can be detrimental to our levels of motivation and awakeness as well as our ability to calm down when we become escalated. Neurofeedback is one fabulous tool that trains our brainwaves back into a more balanced state. With it, we see monumental improvement in cognitive health, emotional regulation, focus, and behavior in individuals who make it a point to tend to this piece of neurological human wellness.

And the brain is just one part of our body's electrical system. Think back to high school biology and what we learned about the nervous system. It's in charge of carrying billions of pieces of data between the brain and the rest of the body to help us respond, regulate, predict, remind, and protect. Sometimes that information travels smoothly from the sender to the recipient. Other times, this message-sending system becomes influenced by various factors, inhibiting its ability to inform your thoughts, feelings, and responses in an appropriate and proportionate way.

You will feel and show up in the world most authentically like *yourself* when you are able to maintain a tether to an electrically balanced state throughout your brain and nervous system. Think of this well-balanced, homeostatic midzone state as your home base. From it, you can upshift into "speed up and go" mode (*hyperarousal*), or downshift into "slow down and stop" mode (*hypoarousal*) depending on what is appropriate for the situation or moment you find yourself in. In nervous-system talk, this language refers to our *limbic states of arousal*. It works kind of like driving a car: when we notice potential danger, we either speed up, slow down, or come to a screeching stop depending on what will most effectively reduce risk.

When our system senses a risk and interprets it as an appropriate time to react or escape, a lightning-speed unconscious response activates our sympathetic nervous system. In a nano-second, the electrical components of the nervous system send messages between the brain and body, triggering a chemical response. There's a rush of cortisol (the stress hormone) and norepinephrine (a hormone and neurotransmitter that facil-itates the flow of adrenaline). In moments, our body feels like it's kicking into action, revving the engine. We may feel irri-tated or fidgety. We might feel the urge to punch something or yell. Or we may have a strong desire to escape, get out of the room, or run.

The amygdala is a small, almond-shaped part of the brain. Its primary responsibility is to protect us from danger. From an evolutionary perspective, it is one of the oldest parts of our neuroanatomy and sometimes referred to as our "lizard" or "reptilian" brain (because of its survival instincts, not because we are ancestors of lizards). The amygdala's job is to alert the body when there's a need to defend or protect itself. It tries to keep us safe. If hyperarousal is the revving of the engine, the amygdala is the foot that presses the gas pedal down. Once the amygdala sends out the electrical message that the body needs to react, the related chemicals start to flow. This causes our muscles to flex, our breath and heart rates to speed up, and our eyes to dilate, all in an effort to prepare us to defend, protect, or escape. If you suddenly have to swerve to avoid a collision while driving on the highway, you somatically feel a layer of that experience separate from your thoughts and emotions. What is sometimes referred to as an "adrenaline rush" is what you feel during that instantaneous release of cortisol and norepinephrine. Symp-toms of anxiety or rage are other examples of a hyperaroused nervous system.

A couple summers ago, my brother Casey and I took a gaggle of kids on a four-day, three-night backpacking trip near Aspen, Colorado. We were responsible for the safety of six kids between the ages of eight and twelve. The hike was steep, and the oxygen got thinner with every ten feet of elevation we climbed. We got a much later start than we meant to. With headlamps on and the sun going down behind the mountains, we started our hike at about 9 p.m. Our goal was to make it to Crater Lake, which sits at about ten thousand feet of elevation, two miles up the mountain from where we parked. Two miles doesn't sound like much until you are carrying a too-heavy pack on an 11 percent-grade incline of strenuous terrain with six young kids in the dark. We made it to the lake at 11 p.m. We were all exhausted, hungry, and cold.

The kids and I huddled in a cuddle puddle under blankets while my brother walked back into the trees to find flat ground to pitch our tents on. After about ten minutes, Casey emerged from the trees and beelined toward us with a look on his face that told me something was wrong. He reached down to grab the bear spray from his pack laying on the ground next to us. I followed suit, snatched the bear spray from my own pack, and removed the safety. The kids and I stood up and looked in the direction my brother was pointing his spray device.

Staring back at us from the pines and aspens fifteen feet away were two eyes reflecting the light of our headlamps.

In that moment, my body felt like I had chugged five cans of Red Bull. My mind went blank, my limbs were tingling with adrenaline, and I could hear my heart beating in my ears. Hyperarousal at its finest. My system was preparing me to defend and protect myself and my family. I knew from the look in my brother's eyes and his body language that the same thing was happening inside him.

After what felt like five minutes (but was actually more like ten seconds), the light from our headlamps shimmered on something about a foot below the animal's eyes. A tag. On a dog collar. Another hiker must have set up camp somewhere nearby. I'm not sure what it feels like for a dog to be bear sprayed on the face, but that hiker's wandering pup was about two seconds from finding out.

We found a place to pitch the tents, snarfed a bite to eat, then bundled up in our sleeping bags to pass out. We were beyond exhausted. With my daughter cozied up on my right and my son snuggling against me to the left, I laid down to sleep, expecting to collapse into unconsciousness. Unfortunately, sleep was nowhere to be found. Between the stress of getting the kids up the mountain, the tension of struggling to find a place to pitch the tents, and the perceived brush with death by bear teeth, my nervous system was wired up to a ten out of ten. My thoughts, emotions, and physical body were buzzing as though they were plugged into an electrical generator. All three buckets in action. Cortisol, norepinephrine, and adrenaline don't disappear nearly as quickly as they show up in a situation like that. It takes time for everything to calm down, metabolize, and flush out. I was stuck in a state of hyperarousal, even though the danger and distress had passed.

*Hypo*arousal, on the other hand, is a function of the parasympathetic nervous system. Hypoarousal wants to preserve energy rather than expend it. This is also a protective mechanism, like the brake pedal in the car. It sends messages throughout the body telling it to get small, lay low, and slow down. When in a state of hypoarousal, you have a hard time feeling motivated. You may want to be alone and avoid stimulation of any kind. Depressive symptoms are associated with a nervous system that feels stuck in hypoarousal. If you've ever known someone who can't seem to get off the starting blocks, as if they are moving through a swamp of molasses in their life, then you know what hypoarousal looks like.

Eeyore from the Winnie the Pooh stories lives in a chronic state of hypoarousal. He speaks slowly, drags his feet when he walks, and is never in too much of a hurry to do anything. (I hope you just read that in an Eeyore voice.) Sometimes, when I'm coming off an intense moment in life or a period of time that required a tremendous amount of hustle, my system responds by dropping me into a hypoaroused state as soon as it feels safe doing so. I experienced this after an intense four-year period in my midthirties. During those years, I worked a full-time job, raised two young kids as a single mom, and went to grad school in the evenings and on weekends. When that multi-year circus finally ended, I barely left my apartment for a full week. I didn't shower or change out of my sweatpants. I slept a ton. And I was completely unproductive. My parasympathetic nervous system hijacked my body and shut me all the way down, which is one of the potential consequences of failing to utilize self-care and taking enough moments to be calm, still, and relaxed.

These varying states of arousal exist within us at all times. They don't only show up when we are experiencing legitimate danger to our safety. For example, when I get angry or excited, my thoughts speed up and I talk too fast. That's a gas-pedal thing: hyperarousal. When I'm stuck in a state of hyperarousal, I have a hard time slowing down enough to relax or sit still. The revved-up state of being serves me really well if I have a busy day and a lot to get done. But if I don't use self-regulation tools to ease off the gas pedal toward the end of my day, I have a hell of a time falling or staying asleep that night.

Conversely, my brakes tend to take over on Sunday mornings when I have nowhere to be, or I get off the grid to hike and camp. Everything seems to slow way down. When we are sick or recovering from illness or injury, the sluggishness we often experience is a form of hypoarousal. In that case, our body is wise to keep us moving slow so it can conserve energy for healing and recovery.

Both hyper and hypo states of arousal can be extremely helpful. It is a healthy thing to be able to dance between the two with fluidity. When functioning in excess, however, each of them can cause problems and make us feel unlike ourselves. What is typically referred to as depression or anxiety is really the observation of symptoms resulting from chronic stuckness in one or the other state of arousal. The pendulum within some folks swings back and forth between hyper and hypoarousal without being able to settle back into the homeostatic midzone. The medical world has historically called the set of symptoms from this kind of nervous-system activity "bipolar disorder."

As we consider all this talk about states of arousal, get curious. Do a U-turn and self-check yours using a scale of 0–10. A measurement of 0 would be very deep hypoarousal. It would be difficult to feel motivated to function much or at all. A 10 would be hyperarousal to the point of sheer panic, blinding rage, or true mania. The home-base midzone range of homeostasis, where you feel most like yourself, would be roughly between 4 and 6. Where do you land on that scale right now in this exact moment? What people, situations, and environments trigger you to spike up into the higher end of the scale? What drops you down into the low end? And, perhaps most important of all, what's your average in life these days? On this scale of 0–10, where do you most commonly float?

Think about the people in your life. Do you know a few folks who seem to baseline somewhere amid the revved-up range of the scale, in hyperarousal? Others whose average seems to float in the more sluggish states of hypoarousal? And maybe you or someone else who bings back and forth between the two without much time to rest and reset in the midzone?

In regard to levels of nervous-system arousal, the point is not to avoid experiencing either state. These internal responses are protective and informative. We need them. The value in understanding states of arousal and having an improved mindful awareness about where you land on this scale at any given time resides in the witnessing process itself and from there, the learned ability to change the state of arousal you find yourself in.

Keep in mind you may notice accompanying side effects in your three buckets depending on your varying state of nervous-system arousal. Your mind might race and thoughts may become increasingly irrational. Your emotions might get big and feel overwhelming. And your physical body and energy might feel out of whack. Or you may shut down, check out, or feel like sleeping all day. This is all normal, and it makes total sense when you consider what's actually happening throughout that body of yours.

Healthy sleep, good nutrition, and consistent exercise serve as a great foundation, setting you up for better success when it comes to nervous-system regulation. Minimized exposure to distressing people, environments, and situations helps too. Of course, I wouldn't be a very good therapist if I didn't also remind us all about the importance of digital wellness. Minimal screen time and steering clear of antagonistic media will help your nervous system stay in a more regulated state.

There are countless incredible resources available to help us self-regulate when we are in an excessive state of arousal. Meditation, mindfulness practices, breath work, yoga, going for a walk, taking a cold shower, exercise, and being in nature are all proven, effective nervous-system regulators. Mindful breathing is one of the most researched and effective ways to moderate states of arousal because it reminds the nervous system we are not actually in danger. Regulation practices can look different from person to person. Aromatherapy, dance, prayer, or meditation may be great for one person, whereas going fishing, playing the guitar, or looking up a new recipe and cooking a meal in the kitchen may feel very regulating to someone else. Consider what works for you and have some healthy options in your back pocket. The goal is to maintain no more than an arm's-length distance from the home-base middle ground between the two extremes of limbic arousal. That way, you never have to stay in a dysregulated state for very long.

Now, when you are feeling out of control, you can remind yourself, "I'm not crazy." Those whacky occasions, while sometimes uncomfortable and perhaps of consequence to the way you feel and function, are totally normal. They are a great reminder that your nervous system is online and trying to take care of you. The next time your family, friends, or colleagues are wondering why you aren't acting like yourself, just tell them, "I'm in a dysregulated state of nervous-system arousal."

Don't unpack your suitcase and live in the dysregulation. Rather, notice it, name it, and give yourself some grace. Use your introspective tools and a healthy dose of curiosity to identify what your system needs to get back into your midzone. And don't be afraid to ask for help from people you trust. As beings who *all* experience peaks and valleys in our psychological wellness, remember, we're in this together.

Everyone has trauma. Everyone. Either you are a robot, or you have trauma. Unprocessed trauma can make us reactive. Neurobiological predispositions or physiological injuries can certainly play a role in reactivity too. But cognitive, emotional, and behavioral reactivity to psychological triggers can often be chalked up to distress-related things we've previously learned,

Trauma

witnessed, or experienced. Reactivity affects our relationships, how we respond to stressful situations, how we make decisions, and about a billion other things. It plays an influential role in how we perceive other people and interpret the world around us.

If you want to feel and function as your authentic self, you've gotta rumble with your trauma. Skipping this part is not an option. If you avoid the traumatic pieces of your puzzle, you will show up in the world as a watered-down version of your truest self, at best. Traumatic buildup is like plaque on your teeth. It is impossible to be holistically healthy unless and until your traumas are identified and tended to.

Mainstream connotations of the term "trauma" miss the mark and make it sound way more scary than it needs to be. In the world of psychotherapy, trauma refers to any event or prolonged or recurring pattern of events that activates your stress-response system. There is a gigantic spectrum of traumatic severity in terms of distress as well as degree of negative impact. The distress can be obvious or obscure. It can be grandiose or subtle. It can come in all forms: physical, medical, sexual, relational, spiritual, or financial. Trauma can result from a transition in life or a loss of some sort. Breakups and divorces certainly qualify as traumas. Right now, as I am writing this book, we are in the middle of the COVID-19 global pandemic. It has ignited a vast array of economic, educational, societal, and political traumas. A trauma can be an identifiable incident, such as a car crash. Or it can be a camouflaged undercurrent of dysfunction, such as growing up in a family where the kids are considered disappointments if they don't have impeccable manners and straight-A grades. Trauma can be the result of neglectful parenting as well as enmeshed, overly involved parenting. Trauma can affect individuals, couples, families, communities, and even entire cultures or races. If something evokes a stress response within you (regardless of whether the stress is rational or not), it has the potential to wiggle its way into your psyche and plant roots in the form of trauma.

When we refer to trauma, most people assume we are talking about a catastrophic event, death, injury, or negative, life-altering situation. For the most part, this assumption covers what we refer to as *big-T* Traumas. A big-T Trauma is a distressing incident during which there is a real or perceived threat to life or safety. Physical violence, auto accidents, and catastrophic natural disasters are all examples of big-T Traumas.

A commonly misunderstood and sometimes minimized type of trauma is known as *small-t* trauma. Small-t traumas include distressing experiences that don't necessarily involve a real or perceived threat to life or safety. Sometimes, they are less obvious traumas and can be hard to identify as traumatic. The loss of a job, for example, can be a small-t trauma. This category can also include things like a difficult postpartum experience, bullying, learning your spouse has been having an affair, or breaking a leg in a soccer game. Retirement or moving from one home to another can be highly traumatic for some people. In the summer before I started fourth grade, my family moved from one side of town to the other, and I changed schools. The new home, neighborhood, and school were all higher in quality and safety than the ones I left behind. But the transition itself was scary to me. It for sure invoked a stress response that lasted for months after the move. The new environments were unfamiliar, and I didn't know anyone. For multiple weeks at the start of the school year, I sat at my desk and cried every single day. For me, this was an example of a small-t trauma situation.

The differentiation between "big" and "small"-T implies one has the capacity to be more problematic than the other. In reality, there is no consistent difference in how much distress or lasting effect a big-T event can cause compared to a small-t event. In fact, a small-t trauma can feel *more* destructive and create *more* problems than a big-T Trauma. Emotional abuse is a great example of this. Long-term psychological and emotional abuse can wreak havoc on the psyche of an individual, more so for some than even a single-episode car accident, for instance. Witnessing or hearing about someone else's experienced trauma, a phenomenon known as *secondary trauma*, is another example of small-t that can have profound negative effects. Medical professionals, social workers, therapists, and teachers often feel the effects of secondary trauma.

Post-Traumatic Stress Disorder (PTSD) is another term that deserves to be addressed. Much of the education and training of mental health practitioners is based on this big, thick book called the Diagnostic and Statistical Manual of Mental Disorders (DSM). It contains hundreds and hundreds of diagnoses along with lists of symptoms that categorize a person as a candidate for specific kinds of treatments and health insurance coverage.

The DSM-V-TR diagnostic criteria for PTSD require exposure to actual or threatened death, serious injury, or sexual violence. These examples are, of course, traumas. This version of the DSM, however, does not account for the impact of more complicated or less obvious types of trauma. At the time that I'm writing this, there is a big push in the mental health industry to update the DSM to account for developmental, attachment, and complex traumas. These issues account for the vast majority of what I see walk through my private-practice doors. They are often far more convoluted than what the DSM-V-TR's description of PTSD accounts for. This adjustment to the DSM would cast a much wider and more appropriate net to encompass all forms of trauma.

Regardless of how much or what kinds of trauma we've experienced, there is one common theme in how it will affect our lives.

This is the lynchpin that determines our potential for healing: **traumatic experiences get stored inside us in a completely different manner than non-traumatic experiences.**

There is a tsunami of sensory components involved in every one of our life experiences. Details of our surroundings (including, but certainly not limited to, sounds, colors, smells, voices, facial expressions, and physical feelings) combine with thoughts and emotions (both our own and those of others). It's sensory chaos. In the heat of a distressing moment, if we consciously considered and tried to process all that information, we would drown in a sea of overwhelm. In moments of significant stress, it is truly not in our best interests to fully process what's happening. A six-year-old kid who gets pushed around by his alcoholic father doesn't have the contextual understanding, cognitive or emotional maturity, or psychological capacity to make sense of what is happening or why. A woman who suffers a pregnancy miscarriage around the same time she finds out her husband is having an affair might unconsciously bury or compartmentalize pieces of one or both of those traumas so she can wake up each day and somehow continue living life. The trauma pieces (whether cognitive, emotional, or physical) that get compartmentalized or avoided burrow into our minds, bodies, and spirits, and create psychological buildup. Over time, the layers of this stuff compound and manifest in all kinds of funky ways.

When my house is a mess but company is arriving soon, I don't have time to strategically organize or deep clean. So, in a pinch, I find the nearest closets and storage bins where I can hide the mess until I have the space and time to efficiently fix the chaos. Because efficient processing of a trauma is not possible in the moment, we unconsciously shove many of the details of that chaotic experience into our innermost metaphorical coat closets so we can wake up, live another day, and keep moving forward. This kind of compartmentalization is a natural and necessary psychological protective mechanism. It's a good thing. Just don't forget the mess remains socked away and will stay burrowed in our psyche until we revisit it later for some spring cleaning.

Over time, we shove distressing mess after mess after mess into the closet. Eventually that door can't stay shut. The mayhem inside starts to grow mold, attract rats, and leak out through the cracks. It puts pressure on the door and its hinges until things start to buckle and break. If one thing in life triggers that door to open a crack, a whole big mess starts to fall out and cause problems. Instead of a junk drawer or coat closet, our trauma experiences pile up in our minds, emotional spirits, and physical bodies.

Wild animals seem to have this figured out way better than us humans. Robert Sapolsky is a neuroendocrinologist and professor at Stanford University. He looks like a slightly older and more distinguished version of Zach Galifianakis's character in *The Hangover,* and he is frickin' brilliant. Sapolsky is also a research associate at the National Museums of Kenya, where he spends time each year studying wildlife, specifically animals' responses to stress. In the mid-1990s, Sapolsky wrote and published a book called *Why Zebras Don't Get Ulcers.* He explained that when zebras experience a traumatic event, they immediately metabolize the trauma by allowing their bodies to go into a conniption of bucking, rolling around, making sound, and running. The animals intuitively know to break down and flush out the internal tension and the cortisol and norepinephrine molecules. They move all the way *through* the distressing experience. This supports the zebra's ability to get back to a state of calm quickly and effectively.

Humans aren't as intuitive as zebras. We usually do the opposite. Rather than doing the work to fully process and discharge trauma, we let distress consume us. Or we numb it, distract from it, blame someone for it, avoid it, minimize or justify it, or run away from it the first chance we get. Then the pain stays inside us and accumulates over the years. All that unprocessed stress piles up and gets sticky, like psychological scar tissue, and becomes unconsciously injected into our thoughts, behaviors, and emotions. It physically stores itself away in our fascia, muscles, joints, and nervous systems. Over time, it can manifest in the form of:

- ✓ distorted beliefs about ourselves, others, or the world at large

- ✓ overwhelming emotions

- ✓ difficulties making decisions

- ✓ dissociative episodes of disconnection from our own minds, emotions, and bodies

- ✓ destructive and unhealthy choices or behaviors

- ✓ obsessions and compulsions

- ✓ physical distress, such as headaches, stiff joints, chronic pain, heart palpitations, vertigo, restless limbs, lethargy, muscle tightness or weakness, fatigue, digestive issues, chest pain, and nausea

The fact that our system knows how to bury distress isn't necessarily a bad thing. This phenomenon is a protective mechanism that keeps our "lizard brain" amygdala from taking over. If the amygdala were a person, she'd be full of urgency, very protective and quick to react, even when she doesn't have all the information. She would be a little bit narcissistic in the sense that she'd be closed-minded and believe her needs immediately and unapologetically over-shadow those of anyone or anything else. The amygdala is great to have around when there's real danger because she doesn't hesitate. She knows how to take charge and make flash decisions. If you know a real person like this, you under-stand what I mean when I say these kinds of characters come in handy in a pinch but can also be a real pain in the ass. They have the ability to make everyone around them feel anxious and stressed with their intense energy.

There are some interesting dynamics between the amygdala and the prefrontal-cortex area of your brain, which is right behind your forehead. In contrast to the reactive amygdala, the prefrontal area is Winnie the Pooh. He's even-keeled, thought-ful, and not reactive at all. Pooh Bear is good at putting ideas together, considering various perspectives, and using data and information to calculate and analyze in a logical way. His efforts revolve around emotional regulation, learning, communicating, and making sense of things. He is much more adept at thinking his way through situations than his intense, reactive colleague, amygdala. This prefrontal cortex area can become quite busy but doesn't (in and of itself) cause us to jump the gun, spout off at the mouth, or respond with knee-jerk reactions. That inten-sity stuff is more amygdala's style.

We can't talk about trauma without also exploring the role of memory. Because it has the potential to block you from feeling and functioning like your most true and authentic self, it is important to understand the relationship between traumatic experiences and the way we store and retrieve content through the complex system of memory. Try the following visual exercise.

Imagine you are out for a walk on a little neighborhood trail. You are feeling calm and relaxed, taking in some fresh air and minding your own business. Imagine you come around a curve and see an object coiled up on the trail ahead of you. The thing starts to make a rattling noise, then uncoils as it raises its head. You notice it has red eyes and horns on its head and is baring sharp, fanged teeth dripping with venom. It's a deadly cobra rattler devil snake, obviously. Okay, I'm being dramatic. Even so, notice what would occur inside your body if this really happened. Feel that adrenaline? Notice that little surge of intense energy? That's your amygdala doing her thing.

Within milliseconds of your eyes intaking that coiled up, angry-looking object and your ears hearing the rattle, the amygdala instantaneously checks this incoming information against her memory banks from your life's history. Based on her files of memories from books you've read, movies you've seen, stories you've heard, and experiences you've lived, the amygdala recognizes the slithery, coiled-up object with fangs as a snake. She recalls that snakes are sometimes unfriendly and have the potential to be dangerous. Instantaneously, your amygdala goes from taking a nap to being wide awake and fully activated, "Oh shit, this is a snake. Snakes can hurt you. RUN!" or "KILL IT!" or "DON'T MOVE A MUSCLE!" She has zero interest in giving the prefrontal cortex even one second to think its way through this situation. She is certain any ounce of wasted time will give the snake the opportunity to strike. She doesn't care what that prefrontal cortex Winnie the Pooh has to say. She shoves him out of the way and reacts to protect you. Phew, that was close! Thank goodness for amygdala!

Fast forward in time, maybe ten years. Imagine you are out for another walk. The environment may even be totally different than the first time. Once again, you turn a corner and notice a coiled-up object on the sidewalk a few feet ahead of you. Amygdala isn't stupid. She knows this scene. She is proficient at dashing through every memory file to recover what's happened in the past. She remembers. Danger. Amygdala opens the floodgates of cortisol and norepinephrine to help your body react. She sends immediate messaging through your nervous system, telling your eyes to dilate, your heart rate to increase, and your muscles to constrict. You jump. The person you are walking with laughs at you because you just startled in fear at the sight of a garden hose. This time a neighbor had been watering his flowers and had accidentally left his hose coiled up on the ground.

So what happened here? One or more details about the current situation reminded your amygdala of something scary or stressful from the past. Those details are what we refer to as "triggers." A trigger is the thing that sets off the amygdala's mouse trap, causing it to snap into action. The mouse trap doesn't care whether the trigger is an actual mouse or a benign feather that happened to fall on it. The shape of the coil and the fact it was lying on the ground in your path was all the amygdala needed. She shoved the prefrontal cortex out of the way (along with its logic, calm, and rationale) so she could defend and protect you. Old, thoughtful, prefrontal Pooh Bear would have paused long enough to breathe and consider what was happening and realize this coil wasn't a snake at all. It was just an old watering hose. But because the amygdala's whole job is to protect you, she doesn't give Pooh the chance. He'd take too long. She's the mouse trap. She's all about action.

By watching neuroelectrical activity, we can visibly see "triggers" creating activity inside the human brain! As we move through our daily lives, our prefrontal cortex is usually lit up like a Christmas tree with energetic activity. But when a trigger occurs and the mouse-trap amygdala activates, it looks like the plug on the Christmas lights of the prefrontal cortex gets yanked, and the amygdala (farther back in the brain) lights up like it's on fire. That neurological phenomenon and the domino effect of physiological, emotional, and behavioral reactions that follows is what we call "trauma response."

Trauma response is protective, and it happens all the time. It's why we jump at scary movies. It's why we slam on our breaks or swerve when the car in front of us stops suddenly on the highway. It's why we may drop our head when someone yells at us or go into defensive mode when someone criticizes us. It's why we instinctively grab for the arm rests when we hit turbulence during a flight.

Trauma response is the reason we check our boyfriend's phone for suspicious text messages even though he's never given an ounce of reason to worry he's being unfaithful—rather, it was our *ex*-boyfriend who had a nasty habit of flirting with other women via text. Trauma response is why some of us low-key always worry about money, even though the bank account is in great shape, because we grew up in a home where financial safety and secu-rity were not the norm. And remember, just because distress-ing information picked up from past experiences isn't an actual threat to life or safety, doesn't mean it can't cause the mouse trap to be any less trigger happy. Subtle undercurrents of unhealthy schemas in our families of origin, maladaptive beliefs we picked up through societal messaging, and seemingly small-potato distressing events can create triggers equally as disruptive as those that result from big-T Traumas.

The final concept to understand about traumatic experiences is that they forever leave fingerprints within us. Trauma has the capacity to chip away at our clearest and healthiest cognitive, emotional, physical, and behavioral functioning. It alters us. The remnant soreness and scars, if we don't tend to them, can fracture our sense of self. They can make us believe we aren't who we used to be or we don't have the capacity to live the lives we once believed we could. They can trick us into thinking we might never be able to feel like ourselves again. Trauma has the ability to deconstruct a loving belief about ourselves, other people, our future, and the world around us. It changes us. If we aren't mindful and inten-tional about tending to our traumatic wounds and integrating our past experiences into our present-day selves, a thick fog will keep our authenticity from being clear and fully accessible.

Your traumatic experiences may be at the root of your biggest pain. But they also may hold your greatest lessons and opportu-nities for healing, growth, and change. This is what Rumi meant when he so famously said,

> *Let a teacher wave away the flies*

And put a plaster on the wound.

Don't turn your head. Keep looking at the bandaged place.

That's where the light enters you.

As you float back through your life and begin to identify sources of trauma, call on local resources that specialize in trauma reprocessing. You aren't expected to know how to rumble with your trauma all by yourself. We are learning more every day about how to efficiently and effectively treat psychological trauma and trauma response through therapeutic modalities like eye movement desensitization and reprocessing (EMDR), body/energy work, neurofeedback, somatic movement methods, and psychedelic-assisted psychotherapy. Find a qualified trauma-informed healer and get to work.

Hardships grow our resiliency and expand our tolerance for difficult experiences. Brokenness reminds us of our humanness. Pain is the conduit for connection to others through empathy. These are beautiful byproducts of unfortunate past wounds. Now your trauma has the potential to be a great educator and catalyst for change. You just gotta be willing to move in closer and get curious. Then work with what you find. Since unprocessed trauma has the ability to influence your neurobiology and hijack your sense of calm sensibility, it shouldn't be left sitting in the dark corners of your psyche. Find it, name it, ask for help, and create shift and healing. Trauma work is not for the faint of heart. It requires a tremendous amount of courage. It is painful. But it's a clean pain. And the freedom experienced on the other side of trauma reprocessing is priceless.

I was introduced to the concept of *multiplicity of personality* early in my psychotherapy career. The first time I was exposed to it, I felt like I was hearing my own native language for the first time in my life. This is a shared sentiment among many of the people who study Internal Family Systems (IFS), a therapeutic

Multiplicity of Personality

modality and life construct developed by Richard (Dick) Schwartz. Nothing about the way I live, work, engage in relationships, parent, or move through the world has been the same since.

Schwartz is a therapist, author, and genius. He spent part of his career as a family therapist, specializing in helping people identify and heal brokenness within their family system. Any good family therapist understands the importance of honoring each individual family member's unique values, opinions, thoughts, and feelings, no matter how different they might be from person to person within the family. When power struggles create a lack of harmony within the system, it becomes unbalanced and lacks trustworthy and empowering leadership. Unity is only accomplished when there is an empathetic and compassionate witness present. This person must be willing to hear, respect, believe, and advocate for each individual as they disclose their experiences. In a family system, that sometimes doesn't exist, resulting in the need to bring a third-party helper (like a therapist) into the mix.

When working with individuals, Schwartz noticed he would often hear people say, "Part of me feels," this certain way, "but this other part of me feels differently." Magical things started to happen when he encouraged his clients, "Tell me more about those parts and why they feel the way they do." He became the empathetic witness for people's separate, varied, and often diverging internal *parts*. What Schwartz discovered is the parts of individual clients seemed to respond to that sincere curiosity much like individual family members would in family therapy. When given the opportunity to have a voice, these parts were often willing to explain why they influence the individual's behaviors in certain ways. Furthermore, he started noticing each part had good reason to feel, believe, and function the way it did within the contextual material of the individual's life experiences.

Schwartz began to conduct therapy for individuals with approaches similar to those he had used in family therapy. Except instead of honoring and bearing witness to each separate family member and their experiences, he did it for the individual's various *parts*. He regarded each part as a separate entity of the person's personality, unique members of an *internal family*. By using nonjudgmental curiosity with the parts, Schwartz discovered they would often provide a tremendous amount of insight and wisdom. But he found this would only happen once the parts felt seen, heard, understood, and respected. He also found that by teaching clients to regard their own parts in this way, individuals learned to be a compassionate witness to their *own* system.

As each client's parts became more responsive and interactive, Schwartz observed a growing sense of inner peace and harmony within their psychological ecosystem. These people were *healing*. Their maladaptive behaviors and thought patterns decreased. People reported feeling improved calm and higher levels of cognitive clarity. Their reactivity went down, confidence went up, and ability to extend compassion and healthy accountability toward themselves and others was established and *increased* as more time went by.

Now IFS has been adapted into a structural modality and is taught and used all over the world in schools, business settings, churches, community groups, nonprofit organizations, wellness facilities, and therapy centers. Research and personal testimonies support the idea we all have this system of parts within us, and by learning to build a relationship with that internal system, we are able to function in better alignment and integrity. Through this, we heal and ultimately feel more like ourselves. That's the whole point of IFS.

As you dive into your personal system of parts, remember you are not your thoughts. You are not your emotions. You are not your physical sensations. Rather you are the *observer* of these cognitive, emotional, and somatic experiences. You are also the witness of your behaviors and reactions. These things are the vehicles through which your system of parts attempts to communicate and take care of you. Your job is to be mindful and curious about what they have to say and show you, then learn to meet their needs and lead your whole system in healthy ways.

If you were interviewing for a new job and asked to talk about a few of your strengths, what might you say? Think about that for a second and write down three of your strengths in a notebook or your journal.

There is a good chance you just identified three of your internal *parts*.

Now let's pretend your interviewer asks that old go-to question, "What is one personality trait you'd consider to be a weakness?" Write that answer down in your notebook too. It's likely a different, distinct part of you.

You should have four things written down: three "strengths" and one "weakness." For each of your three "strengths," answer the following questions:

✓ How long has this been a part of you?

✓ Where did this part come from? (How did you learn it? Was it modeled for you? Taught to you? Or did you adopt this trait because you saw or heard what bad things might happen if you didn't have it?)

✓ What kinds of things have reinforced and/or rewarded this trait? Why did it feel helpful or necessary?

✓ What happens when this trait overfunctions and can't chill out?

✓ What negative, uncomfortable, or scary things might happen if you were completely without this particular trait?

Now consider the "weakness" you jotted down and answer the following questions:

✓ How long has this been a part of you?

✓ Where did this part come from?

✓ How does this trait cause you trouble, distress, or conflict when it overfunctions?

✓ What's potentially *good* about this trait when it's not overfunctioning?

✓ What might happen if you were completely without this trait?

I'll do some of this exercise along with you, as an example. One of my strengths is that I'm extremely independent. I call this component of my personality my Little Miss Independent part.

How long has she been a part of me? My Little Miss Independent part was around prior to high school, but about ninth grade is when I remember her really coming to life in a big way.

Where did she come from? My mom was pretty independent and juggled a lot of responsibilities, so I learned by watching her. I had a significant amount of commitments in my teen years (school, jobs, competitive dance) and was responsible for keeping all the plates spinning. My mom was often busy working at her job, managing our household, taking care of my little brother, and tending to my dad. (My dad lived with us but struggled with alcoholism and was not especially interested, engaged, or helpful in my life.) My Little Miss Independent part helped me meet and manage my own needs and responsibilities. She helped me function at a high level so I could, for the most part, take care of myself.

How was this level of independence rewarded? My mom, teachers, employers, and dance instructors were pleased with Little Miss Independent. I was applauded when I took care of things without needing anyone's help. It was considered admirable. By functioning at a high level, Little Miss Independent also helped me avoid annoying, inconveniencing, or triggering conflict with my dad.

What happens when my Little Miss Independent part overfunctions? Oh man, when she's moving at full force, sometimes she creates the unintentional side effect of pushing people away. Little Miss Independent often refuses to let other people help me. She prompts me to take on more than I can handle on my own. Then I end up feeling overwhelmed and isolated.

What might have happened without Little Miss Independent? My dad frowned upon any kind of neediness. My perception was he didn't want to be bothered. I didn't want to upset him, so my Little Miss Independent part tried really hard to never need his help or attention. I never wanted to add to my mom's stress, so I tried not to need her very much either. Little Miss Independent didn't want me to ever be a burden or the cause of someone else's stress or inconvenience.

During my young adulthood, when I was asked about a personal "weakness" in interviews, I always said the same thing: perfectionism.

How long has this perfectionist part been around? This part started early, roughly around the age of ten.

Where did this part come from? Perfectionism was probably birthed in the dance studio, particularly in technique and ballet classes. I was taught and believed there was a "right" way to do things and a "right" way to look. Hair pulled back, pink tights, black leotard, toes pointed, legs turned out from the hip, belly in, chin up, tail tucked under. My perfectionist part also convinced me she combated chaos. Between my hectic schedule and various responsibilities combined with the complex dynamics resulting from my parents' dysfunction, I had a fair amount of pandemonium in my life. So my perfectionist part came onboard to help me reduce that disorganized energy wherever possible.

Has this part ever caused me trouble? Yes. My inner perfectionist is extremely attached to things being precisely a certain way. When things go wonky, I used to feel tremendous amounts of anxiety. This part helps me feel a sense of control. Another downside is I sometimes feel stressed or become upset when other people do things differently than I would. My perfectionist part sometimes has a hard time keeping her mouth shut, which can offend people.

What is good about my perfectionist part? When she's not over-functioning, she's really helpful! She's extremely handy with organization, which is important as a business owner and a mom. She hits deadlines and keeps our busy family calendar up-to-date. She helps keep the systems in my life running smoothly, like a well-oiled machine. My perfectionist part is great at beautifully decorating a Christmas tree and making the bed in just the right way every morning.

What might happen without perfectionism? If I didn't have my perfectionist part at all, my life would feel messy and haphazard. My children would feel stress because they would miss activities. They wouldn't have the correct resources, like school supplies, when needed. Household bills wouldn't get paid on time. My business would be in shambles. My house would be a disaster, and the bed would never be made, which would totally stress me out. There would be tremendous disorder. I know what chaos feels like, and I don't like it. It reminds me of how things felt inside myself and, at times, in my home when I was a kid. Chaos makes me feel unsafe.

There are two critical things to understand about parts. First, there's no such thing as a bad part.

All parts are good. All parts are welcome.

We know this to be true because of the second important point:

All parts are trying to help us in some way.

If you answered the questions, you were likely able to identify how each of your parts is helpful. Perhaps you were also able to recognize how they can bite you in the ass when they overfunc-tion. *All* parts have beautiful things to offer us as long as they don't function in the extremes. The notion that there are *no bad parts* is going to become hard to believe when I name some other common parts here in a minute. But stay with me, people. I'll explain.

When we first dive into parts work, we usually notice a strong feeling of either appreciation or dismay toward the part. That's why we make the mistake of labeling them as either a "strength" or "weakness." The barometer for how each part resonates with you can be measured by answering the question, "How do you feel toward this part?" As you grow to be more curious about each part and achieve a greater understanding of it, you real-ize they *all* have the capacity to be helpful and useful. You also discover that all parts, when they go overboard, can be disrup-tive and damaging too.

Years ago, when my kids were little, I thought it would be a good idea to show them the movie *Gremlins*. Not my best momming moment. I had forgotten how creepy and violent those crit-ters are. About thirty minutes into the movie, we turned it off and proceeded to stay up late with our youngest son, who was afraid he'd dream about Gremlins coming to get him while he slept.

In the movie, these creatures all start as sweet, fluffy, little Gizmos. They look like a cross between a yorkiepoo puppy and a Furby. The Gizmos are friendly and helpful. But when they eat too late at night, real bad things start to happen. If the Gizmos eat past the stroke of midnight, their skin starts to boil. Their ears and noses grow long, and all their snuggly yorkiepoo fur is replaced by scales and slobbery slime. Their teeth and claws become sharp, and their bodies stretch out into (what all us kids of the 1980s remember as) Gremlins. The Gremlins create problems. They are ornery, violent, mischievous, mean, and destructive.

Our parts are like the Gizmos. They really do want to help us. Often, they come onboard early in our lives because they meet a need. That need might come from lessons we've learned by watching our parents or figuring out what others find admirable. Other times, we onboard these parts because we have no choice. They can come into play to help keep us safe or garner us attention. Some parts do their thing because it helps us avoid pain. Although many of our parts develop during childhood, we can pick them up later in life too. Regardless of when it happens, they all enter our personality and do their thing because *they believe they are helping us.*

Then along come the triggers. Psychological triggers are the late-night snacking that turns the Gizmos into Gremlins. The bigger the trigger, the more overfunctioning the part becomes.

I struggled a great deal (especially in my twenties and early thirties) with a defensive part of myself. Considering the general climate of our current societal culture, an inner defensive part is common for most of us. Mine onboarded when I was a kid, partially from watching my parents argue. Defensiveness was a familiar character in our household. I had insecurities around my own lovability, so I welcomed that handy defensive part and put her to good use. My inner defensive part's number-one job was to protect me from feeling irrelevant.

She knew this insecurity was heavy on my heart and worked to protect its fragility.

My defensive part can be relentless. She used to fight like hell to convince others of my relevancy. If someone tried to tell me something I did was hurtful, my defensive part would immediately kick into action and tell them all the reasons why my behaviors were justified. And holy cow, my defensive part was trigger happy. It didn't take much to send her into Gremlin mode. When that happened, she was loud and talked fast. She would clench her jaw, cross her arms, and get a fire in her eyes that in no way resembled my true, gentle nature.

In my midthirties, my therapist encouraged me to try to access some curiosity toward this part. We asked my defensive part questions and worked to understand it a little better. I was pretty resistant to this idea at first. I had a strong aversion to my defensive part. I didn't like her. She had caused some serious destruction in my life. But as I started to look at her through a lens of curiosity, my mind was blown at how hard she had worked (for more than three decades) to protect my vulnerabilities. When I traced her back to a young age, she reminded me about how she stood her ground when some girls in my sixth-grade class bullied me. She reminded me she had learned how to fight back by watching my parents argue. She believed taking a defensive stance in an argument was the norm. It's just what you do.

Slowly the way I felt toward my defensive part began to shift. When she got riled up, it was like watching a kid throw a temper tantrum. But as I worked to understand her better, she started to soften and calm down. I worked to show her all the reasons I didn't need to be so defensive anymore. I was no longer a little kid being bullied. I had started stepping away from relationships where my feelings weren't honored and valued. I came to realize my defensive part was hyper-protective around any chance I might feel dismissed, misunderstood, or (worst of all) that my feelings weren't relevant. The more I worked to understand why my defensive part did her thing, the more she seemed to be willing to cooperate with me. And the more I curated a life surrounded by people who valued my thoughts and feelings, the more my defensive part realized she didn't have to fight so fiercely anymore.

Don't get me wrong, my defensive part still very much exists inside me. More often than not, she sits close by on the sidelines with a sharp eye out for anyone who may try to devalue me in any way. But she has recognized I'm not a little kid anymore. I now have a great deal of clarity about what's okay with me and what's not, and I have a voice I know how to use. Nowadays, she only shifts into Gremlin mode when there is truly a rational and logical need to defend myself or my family. She and I have a mutually trusting relationship. I can simultaneously stay calm *and* harness her power and conviction. She comes through in the form of my bold and clear voice that speaks up when my truth needs to be spoken. She trusts I'll maintain healthy boundaries and stand up for myself when I need to.

Consider your own parts, especially those that overfunction in ways that are disruptive to your life. Spend a bit of time getting curious about their stories, their intentions, their convictions, and their agendas. Try really hard to stay out of judgment. Show up for them with an energy of pure curiosity and see what they have to say.

Exiles

To understand how and why it is true all parts are working to protect us, we've gotta talk about a concept called *exiles*. The word "exile" makes me think of the *Pirates of the Caribbean* movies when the bad guys punish Captain Jack Sparrow by leaving him stranded on a deserted island. Exiles are the emotional experiences that, if we had the choice, we'd likely take out to a deserted island and leave forever so they never again have the chance to cause us pain, discomfort, or inconvenience.

Every one of us has exiles. Many of them. Particular exiles are more intense for some people than others. But for the most part, we can all commiserate on a number of common exiles. Not-good-enough, for example, feels awful. Wouldn't it be nice to never feel that? Feeling unheard, unimportant, ugly, wrong, worthless, unsafe, stressed, overwhelmed, anxious, stupid, depressed, alone, judged, isolated, misunderstood, and hopeless all pretty much suck.

For the most part, exiles are birthed from unpleasant experiences, including trauma. A client of mine recently shared a story about how upsetting it felt when a colleague dismissed an idea she vocalized in a business meeting. I encouraged her to extend curiosity toward the part of herself that was taking this so personally. While mindfully noticing the distress surfacing in her thoughts, emotions, and physical body, she recalled a memory of being rejected by a snarky middle-school friend when she was fourteen years old. Recalling how that experience felt to her fourteen-year-old self immediately brought back the sadness, tears, pain, and belief that something must be wrong with her or that she was unimportant. That was the narrative she'd written about herself to make sense of that friend's unkind behavior. By reexperiencing the emotional and somatic sensations, the client uncovered within herself a painful exile: rejection.

Exiles also form from pain we've heard about or seen others experience, even if we haven't personally gone through it. Grief is an example of that. If you've ever experienced grief, you know how horrific it feels. But even if you haven't known grief intimately, you've heard about or witnessed enough of other people's grief to know how terribly it must suck. Many of us would likely accept a magic genie wish to forever avoid experiencing grief. Almost every one of us has morbid thoughts of what it would be like if our spouse, partner, pet, best friend, or child died. The thoughts alone are enough to cause us significant pain. Real-life grief is an exile for many of us for good reason. It hurts.

Exiles carry the memories of what pain feels like. It's a sacred job, really. In a beautiful way, exiles remind us we are human. Allowing ourselves to revisit and refeel exiled pain equips us with empathic energy. Without truly knowing the discomfort, suffering, and outright agony of exiles, we can't connect in an empathetic way to someone else who is having a similar experience.

Our protective parts, however, don't value exiles in that way. To them, exiles are a raw nerve they must protect. Parts like to poof up around an exile to try and keep all possible antagonists away from it, like tissue and muscles inflaming around a physical injury. Our parts care about us and don't want us to feel the pain that exiles bring.

Take a moment to consider which exiles are particularly intimidating to you. What are your raw nerves? Trace them back. For just a moment, remember the pain. Feel it. Observe it. Notice what happens in your three buckets: the mind, heart, and body. It might help you understand why your parts fight so hard to do what they do for you.

Managers

Our battalion of protective and defensive subpersonalities can be categorized into two types. The first is a cohort of parts we call *managers*. Our managing parts attempt to be the preemptive strike against exiles. They each do their own specific job in an attempt to protect us from having to feel the sting of an exile. A part that fights to establish and maintain a sense of control is a prime example of a manager. "Control freak" parts of our personality try to decrease the risk we'll ever feel the overwhelm of chaos or the discomfort of uncertainty. For a control-based part, you could say these intentions are its area of specialization.

Parts can get pretty specific too. Controlling parts can show up as disordered-eating parts, micromanaging parts, overexercising parts, pedantic or nagging parts, or parts that enforce dominance in relationships. Most of us have parts that minimize, justify, blame, deflect, or avoid. People who struggle with symptoms of (what we've historically called) obsessive compulsive disorder (OCD) definitely know what it feels like to be extremely attached to control. When you look at that particular diagnostic term through the lens of IFS, we identify it as a *part* of the client that is fighting for control. That's a profoundly different approach than saying a person "has OCD," as if it's a head cold or a genetic disease.

If I had a dollar for every client who walked into my office and told me about how their ex-spouse or mother-in-law is a "narcissist," I'd be a damn millionaire. Here's a big, fat truth bomb: *no person is a narcissist.* A person is a person who was once a little kid and an infant before that. Babies aren't born narcissists. Rather, some people develop narcissistic manager parts that ramp up to protect that person in tenaciously inflexible ways. Every single time I've worked with an individual who has been accused of being a narcissist, I've found this part of them does its job because it is valiantly and intensely protecting horrendously wounded exiles of insecurity and unworthiness. When working with those individuals, I have (100 percent of the time, so far) found their narcissistic part is functioning out of a response to something awful that happened to that person when they were young. It is not uncommon to uncover a childhood history that involved the victimization of these individuals by an abusive parent, bullying, or a sexual perpetration. Think of someone you've perhaps considered to be "a narcissist" and chew on that for a minute.

The "strengths" and "weaknesses" you identified in the exercise at the beginning of this chapter are likely managing parts. They do a job for you because they are afraid if they don't, you will be at higher risk of experiencing distress in the form of one or more exiles. Remember when I said that thing about how all parts are inherently good? That's why! Their whole intention is to protect you from feeling distress or ever being hurt like that again.

If you are reading all this and trying to rationalize the notion that maybe you are free from managing parts, you're in denial (which is, in and of itself, a managing part). We all have parts. Lots of them. And while it's true some manager parts have negative traits (bossy, snarky, passive-aggressive, abusive, runaway, or terrorizing parts), it is also true some manager parts can easily be disguised as admirable. People-pleasing or caretaker parts are great examples of this. On the surface, folks with people-pleasing or caretaking parts seem to be the kindest and most altruistic people of all. But when those parts turn Gremlin, they don't get mean or nasty. Instead, they get codependent. They push an individual's self-value and boundaries aside and tend instead to the needs of other people. Codependent parts tend to overfunction in an attempt to avoid painful potential consequences, like conflict, judgment, or abandonment. Parts of this nature work harder at living life for someone else than they do for themselves.

Have you ever heard a mother say something like, "Oh, my young daughter and I are *best friends*"? If so, you're probably hearing the words of a woman with a managing-enmeshed part. I've met mothers with terrible boundaries who refuse to say "no" or enforce structure and rules for their children because they can't stand the thought of their kids being mad at them. People with these codependent or enmeshed types of parts, costumed as "involved parenting" or "doting partner," can be highly damaging. The wounds of rejection, abandonment, or being alone feel really scary and vulnerable to some people. Enmeshed parts think they can't tolerate the pain of disconnection.

Other manager parts, such as workaholism or excessive exercising, can conveniently be sugarcoated to create the perception someone is super committed to their career or fitness. But in reality, these parts are often helping the person stay distracted so they can avoid dealing with their deeper issues. They give the individual a false sense of enoughness or control.

Thanks to the brilliant work of researcher, educator, speaker, and bestselling author Brené Brown, we now know a whole lot about shame. Inner critics and shame are manager parts. It feels hard to believe our inner-critic and shame parts are good in any way. It sure doesn't feel like they are trying to help us! But look closer. Why does our inner critic do what it does? Why does shame so relentlessly try to convince us we are stupid or worthless? Why does it say we are a terrible person, parent, partner, or friend? When our inner-critic or shame parts go into Gremlin mode, they can behave like real assholes. But get curious. What is their actual intention for us? What are they trying to protect us from?

Here's a way to find that treasure of an answer. Close your eyes and picture your inner-critic or shame part sitting across from you. Ask it, "What are you afraid will happen to me if you stop saying such mean things to me?" Don't think about what this part's answer would be. Rather, listen for it. Truly *ask it*. Go on, try it. If you have a burst of new clarity right here, you won't be alone.

These kinds of parts tend to bully us and tell us all the ways we aren't good enough. It's easy to assume these parts hate our guts. But in reality, they are afraid for us. They don't want us to get hurt. These parts know how risky hope or trust can be.

When you get sincerely curious with your parts and send some compassion in their direction, they'll start to give you answers and insight. They might remind you of painful experiences from the past or warn you of intense pain they'd prefer to avoid in the future. If you extend some loving curiosity in their direction, you might be pleasantly surprised at what they have to say.

Firefighters

While managers are the preemptive-strike mechanisms against exiles, *firefighters* are the parts that rush in with sirens blazing when an exile has already surfaced and is causing distress. They do what any good firefighter does: they try to put the flames out. They think like the managing parts in the sense they believe exiled feelings are a threat to us. They don't believe we can tolerate the distress and hurt that gets activated by exiles. These firefighters try to extinguish pain with maladaptive behaviors.

Take the exile of overwhelm for example. When you're overwhelmed in life, what are some of the unhealthy ways you react to that feeling? Some of us drink a bottle of wine or smoke a big, fat bowl of weed. Others turn to porn or sexcapades to take their minds off all the chaos. In situations of feeling profoundly overwhelmed, a person may have a suicidal firefighting part that truly believes ending their life would result in the ultimate relief. If you've ever had a heart-to-heart conversation with someone who injures themself on purpose, you know that self-harming parts are fiercely intentional and protective too.

Once already in struggle, some of my personal go-to firefighting parts tend to isolate and insulate me from any further risk of pain. I shut down, withdraw, spend a lot of time by myself, and avoid returning calls from friends who have reached out.

For some people, addictions are created by an intense need to escape exiles of anxiety, depression, loneliness, worthlessness, or fear. Rage, lashing out, blame shifting, gaslighting, violence, and abuse are all destructive firefighting behaviors. If there is a perceived risk of feeling wrong, caught, or called out, we may have justifying or minimizing firefighting parts that refuse to take accountability for our mistakes. Avoidance and escapism are passionate firefighters. They believe running away from a situation, environment, or relationship is a better option than leaning into it and moving through the exiled feeling.

Take a personal inventory. What are some of your go-to firefighting mechanisms? Get curious enough to become acutely aware and observant of them. This integral piece of becoming *more yourself* requires you hold yourself accountable for your own bullshit. Firefighting parts tend to live outside your integrity and therefore require reconciliation and rehabilitation. When you douse these parts in curiosity, it is possible to better understand their intentions for you. From there, you can work to harness their convictions and partner with them to create lasting healing and change rather than temporary relief and emotional Band-Aids.

As you begin to take inventory of your own inner system, you might notice some parts serve the roles of both manager *and* firefighter. Consider disordered-eating behaviors for example. An individual with rigid behaviors around food might refuse to eat more than a few crackers per day. In this case, the managerial disordered-eating part may be trying to keep the person from experiencing lack of control. When this same person experiences a situation or phase of life that feels chaotic, the same part may show up as a firefighter. Let's say this person goes through a breakup. The restricting, disordered-eating part may fly into action as a firefighter, trying to extinguish the flames of the spiraling pain.

You know you have one or more triggered parts if you can feel any of these agendas around protection forming. *Parts always have an agenda.* It is their biggest distinguishing characteristic. Sometimes their agendas are sneaky, while other times, they are obvious. Parts' pursuits are well-intentioned, but agenda is agenda nonetheless. Being loosely able to identify the roles of these "managers" and "firefighters" is the first step to accomplishing the internal work that will move you toward better alignment. Don't get too hung up on which parts are managers and which are firefighters, especially considering they can sometimes serve both roles. The important thing is you are mindfully aware of your parts and able to identify when one or more of them becomes activated so you don't overidentify with it or allow it to rule your life. Refrain from reacting. Then, proceed by getting curious enough to wonder why the parts are acting up.

My parts rarely show up in isolation. Usually, they run around in gaggles. My control, perfectionist, uber-organized, pedantic, and judgmental parts all like to hang out together. They are like a little gang. When more than one part gets activated at the same time, it can feel incredibly overwhelming. When a client tells me this is happening to them, I explain they are experiencing a "parts party." It is helpful to get out the whiteboard or a notebook and have the client write down all the parts they can feel in that moment. Listing or drawing the parts seems to help sort and simplify the inner chaos. For those of us who have busy cognitive buckets—with racing thoughts and twenty web-browser windows open in our brains at all times—that exercise can be transformative and even relaxing.

Don't worry about the names you initially assign to parts. Sometimes, they will be easy to identify and name (a defensive or withdrawing part for example). But you'll often notice a part's name is more a description of its actions. Before I had a nice, neat name for my escapist part, I used to refer to it as "the part of me that wants to run away from everything and everyone, fly to Tahiti, and be by myself for the next six months." It wasn't succinct, but it was quite an accurate description.

If it's helpful, you can even give your parts real-people names. I once worked with a brilliant young teenager who struggled with an anorexic part. This part was such a bully to her and was constantly telling her how ugly and pathetic she was. This part told the client that nobody would like her if she gained weight. She named this part Regina after the bullying character in the movie *Mean Girls*. I would ask, "How's Regina doing this week?" The client might answer, "She's been a real asshole and won't stop criticizing me every time I look in the mirror." Other days, she'd say, "Regina is actually pretty quiet and chill this week and has given me some room to breathe." Some clients have named their parts after physical feelings, such as "the part that feels like a heavy pit in my stomach," or a psychological experience, like "the sad, dark, shadowy part that feels like a giant storm cloud hanging over my head." There is no wrong way to identify your parts. Your experience of them is the only clarity you need, even if nobody else understands it.

Sometimes parts don't want to be seen. These are harder to get to. A part that uses drugs or alcohol to calm down every night, for example, might hide in the shadows or behind walls of denial. There might even be a whole lineup of parts protecting other parts through justification and minimization. A deeply shy or insecure part might duck behind a pack of bold protectors, such as a part that never leaves the house without a full face of makeup or a loud, outgoing party-girl part. Stefani Germanotta, otherwise known as Lady Gaga, has been vocal and clear on the fact her "Gaga" persona is a crew of parts she developed as a way to make up for more vulnerable parts and exiles of insecurity and self-doubt. Her Gaga parts are strong and bold. They are unapologetically autonomous, unique, and confident.

It is tempting to assume our goal might be to irradiate our parts. But remember, there's no such thing as a bad part. There are only parts that sometimes overfunction. The mission is to develop trusting relationships with our parts and be curious about them without having an agenda of shutting them up or getting rid of them. You'll find when your parts start to feel recognized and respected for their attempts to protect and help you, they gradually start to cooperate with you and function in new, healthier ways. They calm down when they feel understood and seen for what they are trying to do for you. They begin to take a back seat and serve more in a copilot capacity once they learn they can trust *you* to meet their needs in healthy and sustainable ways.

The willingness to U-turn and look curiously inward at our own complexity is a tremendous sign of emotional intelligence. The process will remind you we are all truly doing the best we can in a tricky and far-too-often-painful world. Folks who are brave enough to be introspective tend to be the least judgmental of us all. Those willing to be inwardly curious are among the most compassionate, patient, empathetic, and open-minded people in the world. These are the people who *get it*. They understand. They know that no person or group of people is any better or less than anyone else.

As you begin to do your own exploratory work and acquaint yourself with your own system of parts, you'll find it's almost impossible not to extend the same grace toward others. You'll find a new ability to look at people who have hurt you with the understanding that those people were being led by their parts, not their truest selves. You'll begin to understand yourself on a whole new level. Once that happens, the fog will start to lift, and your path will become so much clearer.

Polarization **happens when more than one of our** inner parts have strong agendas that don't jive with each other. Polarized parts are the culprit for the gridlock we experience when we can't seem to make a decision. It can feel like an internal argument with yourself, typically resulting in a frustrating cycle of second-guessing and immobilization. Polarized parts are what keep us stuck

Polarization

in patterns or life circumstances even though we know we aren't happy. In this chapter, we'll get you equipped to recognize, explore, and move past polarization through inner-parts work.

Life for my family around 2010 felt like being caught in the riptides of a hurricane. Among all the normal chaos of being young adults, having small children, trying to figure out how marriage works, and fighting like crazy to clean up the messes we had made from mistakes throughout the prior decade, I was watching my parents begin to really struggle. My dad's alcoholism had reached a peak. Years and years of failing to take care of himself left his mind and body wrecked. He had to file for disability, which led to an early retirement. My mom was busting her ass working a full-time job and taking care of the house and their two dogs while doing her darnedest to keep my dad from drowning in an ocean of dysfunction. They were still living in Kansas, an eight-hour drive from where my brother and I lived with our own growing families in Colorado.

Mom didn't like being a state away while we raised our babies. She felt like she was missing out on their childhoods. And Topeka, Kansas, was not her favorite place. It didn't have much to offer for the kind of life she wanted to live. She worked and spent time in friendships with people whom she loved very much, but she was tired of being away from her kids and grand-kids. Plus, tending to my dad's needs was becoming more than she could handle on her own. She was growing to resent almost everything about Kansas.

I found out I was pregnant for the second time early in 2010. This would be my parents' fourth grandkid. At the beginning of the summer, my mom and dad drove to Colorado to go with my (at the time) husband and me for our twenty-week obstetrician appointment. As much as my dad loved his three granddaugh-ters, he was having a hard time hiding how much he wanted a grandson. Dad waited in the lobby while my husband and mom came into the exam room with me for the ultrasound. I was so certain we were having another baby girl I almost told the OB not to tell us the gender. Once the black-and-white image was on the screen and baby wiggled into a sprawled-eagle position, it took about two seconds for me to realize we were definitely *not* having another girl. I pointed at the screen, speechless, and cried. One of my all-time favorite memories is the moment I walked into the lobby and told my dad we were having a baby boy. I will never forget the look on his face and tears in his eyes. My dad didn't much like being surprised, and there was almost nothing that could render him speechless. But this news did the trick in the most beautiful of ways. That may have been the moment my mom finally decided they needed to move to Colorado.

From an emotional perspective, the decision to relocate felt clear to my mom. The logistics of it, however, felt comparable to getting a rocket ship full of astronauts safely launched into outer space. She'd need to quit her job in Kansas and, at nearly sixty years old, cross her fingers that she'd be able to find a new gig in Colorado. From a financial perspective, this was especially scary. The country was still trying to recover from the recession of 2008, and Colorado is an expensive place to live. There would be dear friends to say goodbye to, a house to sell, and new living arrangements to make. The past twenty years of their lives had been spent in that house. All their belongings and storage now needed to be sorted, donated, or packed and moved to Colorado. My dad had boatloads of reservations about the move. He wanted to stay in his familiar environment. Change toward something better, something healthier, felt overwhelming to him. He refused to even try seeing things from Mom's perspective. Dad didn't lift a finger to help with the moving process. He made the whole experience an excruciating swim against the current for my mom. It was clear if the move was going to happen, she'd be responsible for every ounce of the work and transition.

Mom's thoughts flip-flopped between a deep desire to be in Colorado and all the reasons why, on paper, the move seemed like an asinine decision. She questioned herself every step of the way. One inner part of her argued that their life in Topeka was predictable. It wasn't awesome, but at least she knew what to expect. The company she worked for loved her and would be a secure place of employment for as long as she wanted to continue working. Her social network was well established. By staying in Topeka, Mom could have dodged Dad's stubborn resistance too. She knew he would fight her efforts every step of the way. It was impossible to deny how attractive it felt to avoid that conflict altogether.

But something deep inside my mom's intuition kept reminding her of how capable and tenacious she can be, especially when something is really important to her. A pro-move part ran a constant ticker tape in Mom's mind of what life could be like living in the same town as her kids and grandkids. She daydreamed of what it would feel like to go to their softball games and dance recitals, be around for every birthday dinner, and be just down the road if my brother or I ever needed last-minute help with the kids. This part played on her mamma-heart, reminding Mom she'd be able to swing by and check on us in person when we got sick or had a bad day at work. She'd get an infinite amount more hugs, get to hear all the little kid giggles, and have the chance to develop closely bonded relationships with all four of her grandchildren. She had missed so much when my daughter and my brother's girls had been little. This part of my mom didn't want her to miss out on those profound moments with this fourth grandbaby too.

I think this part also knew, deep down, my dad's health wasn't going to improve. The future of his physical and psychological wellness was grim. He didn't even want to feel or get better. Mom made a choice and felt convinced she would see this man through the finish line of his life, no matter what. It was becoming obvious she was losing her own okayness by trying to keep that commitment, while living a state away from the people she loved most in the world. This pro-move part knew she needed her family close by as an oxygen tank while she followed through on those last few years of vows to my dad.

This inner battle between the anti-move and pro-move parts of my mom is a textbook example of polarized parts. One side of this tug of war felt ferociously dedicated to getting Mom to Colorado. The opposing side felt scared, intimidated by the process, and exhausted from my dad's resistance. This kind of conundrum is a recipe for stuckness if we don't know how to rumble with polarized parts and find some access to courage and clarity.

It is so important to remember here that there are *no bad parts*. Even the most stubborn or maladaptive of parts still functions out of an attempt to help you in some way. In the most sticky polarizations, we often see we aren't feeling the activation of just two battling parts but rather two or more entire departments of parts that can't seem to agree. It gets complex and can feel overwhelming.

When polarized parts are activated, watch out for a *rubber-band effect*. When we have spent a great deal of time blended with parts of one nature, then hit a snafu that wakes us up to the realization we no longer want to function that way, our inner gears start to grind. The most profound and destructive rubber-band effect I've ever experienced radically altered my presence in the world during the years of my early thirties. By this point, three decades of biased influence from various people, cultural norms, and social messaging told me I should strive to be a "good girl." I had soaked up a perception that to stay safe, loved, and stable, my best bet was to remain quiet and small. Don't rock the boat too much, and refrain from disagreeing with people, especially those in positions of authority over me. Don't have too many needs or wants of my own. And above all, never, ever veer from the expectations that others had imposed on me.

A handful of different factors created the perfect storm by the time I entered my thirties. The thunderheads had been building, and the clouds became too heavy to hold all the pain, tears, resentment, and inauthenticity. I was *over* it. The storm clouds let loose with a ferociousness I didn't even know existed inside me. I was sick and tired of being the daughter, wife, mother, and friend everyone perceived as conforming, conservative, and self-sacrificing. I started waking up to my own wants and needs, my own opinions, and my own desires for life. I craved pursuits some people didn't seem to understand or, in some cases, agree with. I had walked one path for thirty years and come to the edge of a cliff. All the guttural intuition inside me knew I could not keep my sanity while going back down the path from which I came, acquiescing to the expectations of everyone else. This precipice felt like a line drawn in the sand between a lifelong, well-trained submissive side of me versus a newer, polarized, and less-familiar team of parts that valued bold authenticity above all else.

This newfound confidence and autonomy saturated the way I spoke, the things I posted on social media, the thoughts I was having, and the way I treated other people. My overly polite parts were replaced by vocal, overly opinionated parts. Rather than making choices based on what felt best to everyone else, I began putting myself first for a change, with no apologies or exceptions. Instead of stuffing my anger and pain down so other people could stay comfortable, I let my angst be known. I learned to use my voice in such a way that every last person who had ever put me in a box would hear it loud and clear. I was done being polite. I was finished with staying quiet. I refused to be the sweet, submissive girl everyone else expected me to be. Living out of alignment for so long had built up pressure inside me. When I finally allowed my people-pleasing parts to relax, I catapulted with force like a rocket launcher into overfunctioning, ego-driven parts. Combative, point-proving, stubborn parts threw my entire department of codependent parts down into the basement and locked the door.

This created a whole new set of problems. The new, bold bus drivers were no less dysfunctional or damaging than my submissive and codependent parts had been. It took me about three years to even realize what had happened. When I finally woke up and realized how hijacked I had been by this new set of extreme parts, I needed to rein it in a bit. There must be a happy medium between severe codependency and brazen individualism. I had to find a middle ground.

There is a window between polarized extremities that allows for movement in either direction based on what is appropriate in any given moment or situation. It is not a neutral space exactly. Rather, it's an idle position that provides flexibility for leaning into either a submissive energy or a bolder, more egocentric energy. When we can achieve access to this dynamic middle ground, we get to *choose* which way to lean. It's harder for parts to hijack the bus from that midzone.

Just remember, as the rubber band gets stretched tighter and tighter in one direction by parts functioning in one extreme, the potential for intense rebound gets real. The tighter the rubber band, the more tension exists. With more tension comes more risk of excessive polarized reactivity. The rubber-band slingshot has the potential to overshoot the middle window of fluidity and catapult us into the opposing extreme. So, beware. When the parts that have been quieted for too long are finally handed the microphone, it makes sense they are ready to party and raise some hell. But just because it's understandable, that doesn't make it rational. And it doesn't make it okay.

Reflecting on this concept of polarization makes me think of my time spent working in the corporate world. I remember the tension between our creative department and our finance department. Our creative department was known for coming up with brilliantly fresh ideas and thought-provoking, eye-catching, attractive concepts. They used to make our finance folks crazy because there was very little attention being given to budgetary restraints. So finance always had to be the bad guys who reined all the fun creativity back in by setting limits around what was (and wasn't) economically feasible. On the flip side, if the finance department had been put fully in charge, there'd have been a significant deficit in creativity, play, and fun. In this context, it's easier to realize that both departments are necessary in order to generate a successful outcome. Without a fabulous creative team, our events would have been boring and dull. Without the money guys reminding us of our financial limits, we'd have ended up in bucketloads of debt, which would not have been good for the business.

In a similar way, my submissive parts have a ton of value to bring to the table in terms of patience, kindness, and consideration of the needs and feelings of others. My egocentric parts help me with confidence, advocating for my own needs, healthy boundaries, and speaking up about things that feel important to me. When my polarized parts learn to respect each other and *work together*, the cooperation results in me feeling most like *myself*. Therefore, consider your own internal parts as entities of an inner organization, a system. As you begin to listen to the intentions of our parts, then help them see each other's strengths, you establish a sense of harmony within the system. Parts begin to respect each other's abilities to contribute. Harmony and increased synchronization within the system steady the ground under your feet and serve as a much more solid foundation to live, function, and make confident decisions from.

Polarization is a normal part of being human. If we pay attention, we can all notice microcosmic polarizations within us every single day. They show up in the form of the parts that want to fit in a workout versus the parts that want to take a day off and avoid having to shower a second time today. Or parts that want Mexican food for dinner versus parts that recognize it's been a while since we've had a clean, healthy salad.

The conscious observation of the wrestling match between parts is one of the best breeding grounds for personal growth. Nobody is immune to polarization. For instance, recently, one of my young-adult clients moved through some fascinating dialogues between his polarized parts. His fiscally responsible "401K" part wanted him to accept a corporate job, save money for his future, and do the "adult career thing" so he could lay a safe financial foundation. But a polarized "surfer dude" part of him desperately wanted to spend some of his twenty-something years living by the ocean, creating and building surfboards.

Another client mediated between a part of her that wanted to leave a very unhealthy marriage and a part that felt extremely passionate about having babies. She was already in her early forties and afraid if she left her husband, the opportunity to become a mother would likely dissolve with the marriage.

When I feel stuck between polarized parts, I remind myself that if one department of parts contributes 49 percent of how I'm thinking and feeling about something, while another gaggle of parts contributes 51 percent, that's still a decision-guiding equation. It may only be a 2 percent difference, but it's enough to support my intuition with an answer. When stuck between polarized parts, we may never have full clarity and confidence in our choice outcome. In fact, we may be at risk of feeling some level of regret no matter what we choose. Just remember, the other side of that exact same coin is that it's also a win-win. There can't be downsides to both options without also having upsides to both.

Listen to the fears your polarized parts express. Don't be afraid to sit in the discomfort of not yet knowing how things will end up. That special spot of uncertainty will wake you up in new ways. It will remind you of your vulnerable humanness and open more space for personal growth. Be there, courageously, for the rumble between your polarized parts. Honor and communicate respect to each and every part that speaks up. Acknowledge their attempts to help you. Guide them to see each other's strengths and consider a collaborative approach instead of bulldozing to get their own way. Watch out for the rubber-band effect. Without clear and compassionate guidance, the parts that have felt too muzzled for too long carry a power that can be as destructive as the extreme parts they are rebelling against.

Above all else, know this inner circus of parts does not have to be a free for all. There is a ringleader, separate from your parts, who is very well resourced and capable of meeting the needs of *all* the parts using wisdom, calm, and grace.

That ideal and ultimate leader is *you.*

So far, we've established your personality comprises multiple parts. But then, does that mean *you* are just a sum of these parts?

No.

You are something different. You are *yourSELF*. A conscious being with the capacity, capability, and wisdom to

Self

support, compassionately listen to, and lead your system of parts.

In my psychotherapy career, I have worked with individuals who have committed sexual offenses, murder, theft, domestic violence, tax evasion, and insurance fraud. I've sat with people who cheated on their spouses, beat the daylights out of other people, lied to their families, gambled their life savings away, or relied on drugs or alcohol every day for years and years. I have treated folks with symptoms of manic depression, disordered eating, paranoid delusions, self-harm, and suicidality. I've had clients yell at me, swear at me, call me names, throw things at me, storm out of my office, and fire me. And yet, I can sincerely say I have never ever sat with a single human who I didn't believe has a sense of something more, something beautiful, within them. By this, I mean that no human being can be merely reduced to or defined by their parts or simplistic labels, no matter how dark the vice they're driven to. No matter how reactive or disconnected they might be.

This pursuit of becoming *more yourself* is impossible to continue without asking the question: *Who are you?* And what do I mean when I use the word "Self"?

You are driving a bus. A big one with lots of passengers. You are comfortable driving the big vehicle. You've been doing it for a long time. You never have certainty about the obstacles, construction, navigation issues, or bad weather conditions that might pop up. But you've learned through experience to trust yourself. You are confident you are equipped for whatever might arise. So, you're up there behind the wheel, cruising down the road, jamming to your music, making sure your passengers get safely from point A to point B. As you drive, you are awake and aware but relaxed.

One of the passengers from the back of the bus notices storm clouds up ahead on the horizon. He has strong feelings of fear and worry. This particular passenger was on a bus once before that headed into a storm. Bad things happened during this previous experience. The road was slick with rain, and the storm clouds poured out hail and sleet. The storm caused damage to the bus, collisions for other cars, and a major delay in travel. The worst part of that previous experience was how unnerving and scary it had felt. So now, when this passenger sees the storm clouds ahead, he remembers that previous experience and refeels the fear. He stands up, rushes to the front of the bus, shoves you out of the driver's seat, and pulls the bus to a screeching halt on the side of the highway. There's no way this passenger wants to relive the experience from his past or anything like it ever again.

Do you see where I'm going with this metaphor? Each of the passengers on the bus is one of your parts. Some are super chill and content with being along for the ride. The hum of the bus engine and the steady vibration of the road under the wheels seems to relax some of the parts. Some feel excited about the adventure of the path you're driving down. Others have a harder time sitting back and allowing you to drive the bus without their interference. They feel antsy when something about the driving conditions, obstacles in the road ahead, your driving style, or the destination itself spooks them. When these parts feel triggered, they start to chirp at you from their seats in the back of the bus. In some moments, their comments and warnings are subtle. Other times, they are louder, more persistent, and, occasionally, frantic. Then there will be times when providing you with their worried chatter doesn't feel like enough. They can't stop themselves from rushing to the front, commandeering your driver's seat, and hijacking the entire system with their own agenda, panic, and preferred reroutes, reactions, and road maps.

Among the clamor of all these passengers, this metaphor introduces a new character: YOU, the driver. The IFS model refers to this driver as "Self." Self differs from your parts. It is still an entity of the system, but it is separate from your parts. Self is the consciousness able to observe the behaviors and characteristics of the parts. Self is your core identity. It is who you are apart from all the parts. If you believe, as I do, that all people are inherently good, then Self is the embodiment of this. Self contains and emits all the best qualities of leadership. These are known in the IFS world as the eight Cs.

- ✓ calm

- ✓ confidence

- ✓ courage

- ✓ creativity

- ✓ connection

- ✓ compassion

- ✓ clarity

And my favorite:

- ✓ curiosity

When we have unobscured access to these eight qualities, we are able to say with sincerity, "I feel so much like my*Self*." When we are "in Self," it is easier for people to be in relationships with us. Our nonverbals, voice, responses, and general energy are welcoming, relaxed, and open. We make better leaders, friends, and parents when we function from a place of "Self-energy." We are able to receive feedback and even criticism from a relaxed and open-minded place when we are in Self. Self doesn't carry judgment or bias or agenda. It is not second-guessing or insecure. It doesn't even know how to get defensive. Self is easy going and relaxed. Self is innovative. Self is wise. Self is like a completely equipped, very calm, and well-resourced parent.

When is the last time you remember feeling wholeheartedly like *yourself?* Was it recently? Has it been a long time? I feel a pang of empathy whenever someone answers that question with, "I don't even remember the last time I felt like myself." I've been there before, at a point in life when I truly couldn't remember the last time I felt clear and at ease enough to say I felt like *me.*

We might reflect on the last time we were able to take a vacation and step away from our normal daily responsibilities. Certain environments or being around specific people might help us to feel more like ourselves. For instance, my best friend Rooney is one of the few people in life with whom I feel zero obligation to be anything other than just me. She adores me at my best and stays out of judgment when I'm blended with parts or at my worst. Rooney has proven, over many years of friendship, she loves me exactly as I am with no agenda of wanting or needing me to be different. That kind of friendship is a beautiful breeding ground for Self-energy. I have easier access to Self-energy in nature too. Something about sitting by the ocean or hiking through the mountains settles me into a space of needing and wanting nothing other than exactly where and who I authentically am in those moments.

Imagine it's a gloomy, snowy day in the middle of the winter, and you and I are sitting in a room together. Pretend I point out the window and ask you, "What color is the sky?" What would you say? Gray, perhaps. Or white, right? Then imagine me shaking my head and disagreeing, "Nope, it's a beautifully clear, bluebird sky up there." When you look at me with a confused expression, I'd explain my rationale. If you were to get into an airplane and fly up through the fog and clouds, what color would the sky be then?

Blue. Clear blue.

Yes! Gray isn't the color of the sky. Gray or white is the color of the clouds! It's amazing how deceiving those darn clouds can be, making us believe the sky itself has turned gloomy gray. What's real and true is the clouds are blocking the blue sky from our vision. But the sky is always there, always blue, always clear.

The same is true in the relationship between parts and Self. Sometimes your parts can be as convincing as snow clouds, morphing and distorting your view of the blue sky, and Self becomes hard to feel and hard for others to see. You might, for example, perceive yourself as being an "anxious person." Perhaps it's true you show and feel the effects of anxious *parts* that block the calm of Self. But it is not actually accurate to say you are an "anxious person." That blockage is not *you*. It is, again, just a part. An *anxious part*. You, at your core, are calm: one of the eight C words that together make up the eternal flame of unbreakable truth that burns inside you. It never goes out. It never dims. At times, perhaps you believe yourself to be an "insecure person." But it just ain't so. Rather, you may have an *insecure part* with self-doubting thoughts and an influence that makes you drop your head and avoid eye contact. But your true identity is one of confidence, another C-word quality of Self. If you feel anything that keeps you from being, feeling, thinking, or behaving in any other way than in alignment with those eight C words, you are "in part" or "blended" with parts. In those moments, you are experiencing a blockage of Self-energy. The clouds are in the way.

This differentiation between Self and parts throws a real wrench in the diagnostic framework of most mental health practitioners. It is the foundation for my decision to be a non-pathologizing psychotherapist. Again, I do not believe any person is "bipolar" or "an addict" or "a narcissist." Rather, I believe every person is a *person*, a being of light and love, comprising the eight C-word qualities of Self. Any dysfunction we feel, or that is on display for others to see, is a manifestation or consequence of agenda from parts that are blocking Self from shining through. These parts can certainly be influenced and motivated by neurobiology, trauma, culture, our history of attachment to other people, substances, media, injuries, and life experiences. Just remember, their overfunctionality (whether occasional or chronic) doesn't make you inherently wretched. Those parts and their reactivity are byproducts and consequences; they are not *you*.

Tremendous amounts of hope and freedom come from the understanding that Self is *always* in there. It never goes away. It's just really hard to access sometimes. This is so, so, so important to understand in order to combat strongholds of shame or deflection (which are two sides of the same coin). Once we recognize the constant presence of Self, we have no choice but to identify our own part-influenced dysfunction. That observation and ownership is the place where change and evolution are born.

I recognize there will be critics of this perspective. I can understand the resistance to challenging labels. Pathological labeling is convenient. But it can also be separating and othering. When we label ourselves or someone else as "an addict" or "a narcissist," for example, we fail to recognize their humanity. If you've ever loved someone who struggles with addiction, you likely know how hard it is to turn the love switch off, no matter how much pain they have caused you. I have wrestled, multiple times, with the desire to flip that switch and turn *off* my love for someone. I've wished to stop feeling love for my dad when his abuse and addiction caused me so much pain. I've tried so hard to stop caring for a friend, family member, or ex-lover who abandoned or mistreated me. But, no matter how hard I've tried, I still love them all, deeply. Every last person who has hurt me. That's because I know that Self exists within them. It may be buried under layers and layers of pain and maladaptive beliefs and behaviors, but it's definitely in there. So we love them. We can't help it.

Labeling that is based on the influence of our overfunctioning parts gives us permission to consider others as separate from us. It denies our common humanness by creating an invisible curtain between "us" and "them." It is a culturally and socially acceptable vehicle for judgment. It involves the assumption that we don't all struggle with significant repercussions of our own maladaptive parts. Calling a person or group of people a name determined by the prominent symptoms of their most over-functioning protective parts is segregating and dividing.

Instead of relying on a label, consider trying some parts language. For instance, rather than saying, "Ugh, my ex-husband is such a narcissist," try "My ex-husband struggles with narcissistic parts that really influence his thoughts and behaviors." Rather than referring to your boss as a "control freak," try regarding her as having "extremely strong control parts." Give people their humanity back with the perspective that a love-worthy Self resides within them. Because of that, we are all more fundamentally alike than we are different. Rather than cynically calling yourself a "lazy piece of shit" when you aren't feeling motivated, change that internal language to recognize you have some lazy parts that happen to be driving the bus lately. Do you see how that shifts the energy around the laziness? It depersonalizes it, which reminds us that laziness is not all there is to us. It does not define us.

Dropping people into categorical boxes feels good to the rest of us who don't struggle with the same things. It is a way to separate ourselves from "those people." It is far more comforting to believe the man who recently walked into a grocery store in Boulder, Colorado, to shoot and kill multiple people is a lunatic, a crazy person, a demon. We'd rather believe he's a pathology than a person, and we deny we all have the capacity to think, say, and do radically awful things. Judging or disconnecting from people who think or believe differently than us (from a political, religious, or sexuality perspective, for example) is another way we try to comfort ourselves. We don't want to recognize our commonalities because it causes us angst to honor them as human, just like us, worthy of belonging and respect. Labeling and ostracizing people helps us sleep at night, feeling grateful we aren't one of those really screwed-up dirt bags. We do it to make ourselves feel better. I don't know if there's anything more damaging than forgetting our shared humanity in this way. It is highly uncomfortable to admit our own beliefs, opinions, lifestyles, needs, and wants are no more and no less valuable than those of any other person or group of people.

Furthermore, when we label an entire personhood based on someone's overfunctioning parts, we enable them to stay in their dysfunction. We define the wholeness of their existence based on a set of symptoms, as if they are forever doomed to being that certain way. How in the world can we expect people to fully heal or rehabilitate if we've already written them off as holistically and forever broken?

We do it to ourselves too. Someone with a substance reliance might shrug and say, "Once an addict, always an addict," as if it's a lifelong sentence they have no choice about. YOU are not an addict at all. You are *you*, a human. You were a tiny, sweet baby at one point, learning to smile and laugh and bounce to music. There's no "addict" in that. You may struggle with some *parts* of you that rely heavily on substances to minimize the number of minutes you spend in pain and distress. But that doesn't make your core identity that of an addict. Overidentifying with our parts enables us to avoid the pursuit of holistic healing. If we aren't careful, we risk giving ourselves permission to stay in a lack mentality and make excuses for living small. We miss important opportunities to challenge and remedy internal and external systemic brokenness.

You may have an inner critic part that says you're a failure and less worthy or lovable than other people. The thoughts associated with that part don't equate to truth. That mean, critical part of you says what it says for a reason. Maybe it is trying to protect you from taking risks or feeling hopeful because it doesn't want to see you get hurt. Maybe it is trying to motivate you. Maybe it wants to be the preemptive strike against rejection and feels that if it beats other people to the criticisms, the pain won't be quite as awful. Regardless of its rationale (no matter how convincing it feels), *you* are not a failure. *You* are not less than.

As long as we continue to use parts-based labeling to characterize ourselves or anyone else, we risk staying in a place of blame, shame, and non-truth. It makes full healing and rehabilitation a nearly impossible, uphill battle. Overidentifying with parts makes it difficult to access the qualities of pure, altruistic, unadulterated Self-energy.

If the way toward a more joy-filled, fulfilling, purposeful life is to remember *who we are*, identify and rule out who we are *not*, and live more fully in alignment, then labeling others and overidentifying with our own parts cannot be the way we roll anymore. That familiar norm is outdated. It's an ineffective, neurotic paradigm. If you want to feel like *yourself*, and if you want to empower others to do the same, the othering and labeling have to stop. The presence of Self is a global commonality. It is a shared truth that enables us to see a little bit of ourselves in every other person, no matter how different we may seem to each other.

You are calm.

You are courageous.

You are connected (to yourself, to others, to the world around you).

You are clear.

You are creative.

You are compassionate (toward yourself and others).

You are confident.

You are curious.

When using the words "you are" or "I am," take comfort in knowing anything negative that exists outside of those C-word truths is complete and utter nonsense. You may have parts that say otherwise. But that's only because they are looking at the clouds, not the sky.

An "Aha!" moment is one of those particularly sacred instances when newfound clarity creates a shift and reconciliation within the way we perceive or understand something. It's like when you're struggling to finish putting together a puzzle, then suddenly realize you had two pieces mixed up. When

Everything Is Neutral + Nothing Is Personal

you reposition them correctly, it paves the way to the finish line for the whole thing. Wrapping my head around the concept of *ultimate neutrality* and accepting the notion that *nothing is personal* were two of the most impactful "Aha!" moments of my life.

A Course in Miracles, scribed by Helen Schucman, is an interesting kind of book. It's massive, the size of a small stepping stool. It's full of philosophy and theology of the life-changing sort. "This is a course in miracles. It is a required course. Only the time you take it is voluntary." There's a part of me that feels motivated by provocation, so with that kind of stark challenge on the book's first page, this one was game-on from the start.

The first few lessons focus on the philosophy that everything is neutral. A chair is only defined in our mind as something we sit on because of the constructs we've wrapped around it based on our life experiences thus far. The texture of softness is meaningless. The stinky smell of a skunk's spray is a neutral thing. The name we've given to anything is also meaningless. There is no goodness nor badness, rightness nor wrongness to anything. This goes for all foods, experiences, sensations, words, and choices. It is true of places, colors, sounds, and accomplishments. The only reason we assign notions of good, bad, right, or wrong to anything is that we've learned to. Assumptions and labels of meaning are established through the influence of the people we've spent time around, books we've read, society we've lived in, media we've paid attention to, things our parents taught us, and culture that saturates it all with biased insinuations.

If an alien came down from outer space and walked into your home, do you think it would know what the hell to do with a toilet? Or a piece of cake? That alien would perceive these items as completely foreign and meaningless until we offered up descriptions and definitions. This whole notion of neutrality explains why babies aren't afraid of dogs until they get bitten or barked at for the first time. A toddler will grab a sharp knife because he has not yet learned the context surrounding a knife that tells us it might be dangerous. A child isn't born with that knowledge. There's no context until there is. Once meaning has been assigned to something, we file it away in the endless memory bank of our mind and use it over and over again for the rest of our lives until there's a reason to alter it.

I love the scene in *The Little Mermaid* where Ariel combs her hair with a fork. She had never used a fork to eat with before. (Do mermaids eat?) She'd never heard it called a "fork." So when Scuttle the seagull tells her it's a "dinglehopper" and it's used to comb hair, she embraces those pieces of information as if they are undeniable truths and begins to rake the utensil through her long, red mane.

Some serious magic happens when we apply that logic to things in our daily lives. It's a game of perception. We start to recognize that everything means what it means to us only because of the layers of context we've adopted from our previous experiences, the influences around us, or both. The things themselves are actually neutral masses of atoms and tangles of colors, movement, sensation, energy, and sound.

The number of followers you have on your Instagram account—it's neutral. It means nothing. Your clothing size means nothing. There is nothing right or wrong about the sound of a bird chirping. We allow someone who cuts us off on the highway to dictate our mood for the next hour, even though we have no idea about the circumstances happening in that person's parallel moment. We get angry at the sound and energy of someone calling us a mean name but not at the sound and energy of the wind blowing or a bell ringing. Isn't that weird?

Let me give you an example. It's a summer day. The sun comes up and shines bright in a clear sky for the first half of the day.

Then, around 2 p.m., thunderheads take over, and rain dumps from the clouds for the rest of the day.

The rain itself is neutral. The dark clouds, gray color of the stormy sky, and wetness created by the rain are all neutral. If we forget about that neutrality, we give that rain all the power in the world by assigning meaning to it and judging it based on the context of our own life circumstances.

A bride who has been planning and daydreaming about her outdoor wedding scheduled for this day is bound to have some strong feelings about the goodness or badness of this rain. She may have intense adverse emotions about those dark clouds and the moisture from the downpour.

But the farmer down the road has been waiting for a rain like this for weeks. His crops are dehydrated from a recent drought and hot weather. His income and family's livelihood are dependent on days just like this. He has prayed with desperation for this exact weather.

The rain itself means nothing. The meaning we assign to it based on our own contexts means everything. Our perception is the determining factor in how much and what kind of energetic and emotional power we give it.

Here's another example. I worked with a client who felt fiercely convicted about and attached to his political opinions and perspectives. His particular viewpoints differed from what he believed to be the majority consensus of people who live in the state of California. Because of this, he drew a correlation between people who live in California and people who staunchly and offensively disagree with his political views.

The client confided that he felt triggered every time he saw a car with California license plates driving on the road. When he saw Cali plates on a car, this client's heartrate would speed up, his body temperature would rise, and he'd become physically agitated. Feelings of rage and frustration would swirl around in his emotional bucket. And in his psychologically triggered mind, the driver of that car must certainly be some asshole who vehemently stands against everything this client believed to be good, true, and right in the world.

This entire intense reaction was spurred simply by seeing a California license plate.

In reality, it was completely possible the driver with those tags did *not* have political views that differed from my client's at all. That driver might not even be a California resident! They may be someone from Texas, Tallahassee, or Tahiti who rented a car that just happened to have California tags. In the context of this concept that *everything is neutral*, every California license plate was meaningless. They only evoked this intense reaction inside my client because of the assumptions he subconsciously attached to them. His perceptions (regardless of how accurate or inaccurate, rational or irrational they were) colored his entire experience. In the end, he may have been totally right about every driver of every car with California tags. But there is a stronger likelihood he was, more often than not, wrong. The tags meant nothing. They were just metal license plates.

All things are neutral. When we assign meaning and give emotional power to anything, from a social media post to the words someone says to us, we are doing so with an (at least partially) uninformed set of inferences. This is why curiosity deserves a seat at the table, especially if we want to expand our considerations to encompass all possibilities. When our thoughts lack curiosity, they turn into assumptions. Since assumptions are colored by our own biased and extremely limited experiences of the world, they lack a broadened perspective. They are deficient in considering all applicable data. Therefore, they are faulty and unreliable. Dousing these moments with curiosity cracks the whole thing open a little wider so we can more fully understand. It infuses potentially antagonistic situations with a gentler energy and an intention for expansion rather than sticking to stubborn certainty.

Once I started wrestling around with this philosophy that all things are neutral, my second "Aha!" moment slid right into place. Nothing is personal.

Don Miguel Ruiz has written many brilliant books, my favorite of which is *The Four Agreements*. In this book, Ruiz argues everything anyone says or does is a result of their own reality, not yours. Put differently, others see the world, including how *you* show up in it, through a lens clouded and colored by their own completely unique set of life circumstances, experiences, culture, values, and beliefs. They write mental stories and create assumptions about you based on this lens and, at times, without an accurate understanding of your actual intentions or viewpoints. Therefore, their actions and reactions toward you should never be taken personally.

Ruiz reasons that our suffering at the hands of someone else's actions or words is needless and unproductive. If you can remember that all things are neutral and be mindful of the meanings you create, you'll have a better chance of freeing yourself from unnecessary angst. In other words, you'll have better access to Self, resulting in you feeling and functioning more like *yourself*.

There's a great depiction of this in the film *A Beautiful Day in the Neighborhood* starring Tom Hanks. A journalist is writing a story on Mr. Rogers, the iconic PBS children's show host from the 1970s and 1980s, and arguably one of the world's kindest humans. That dude was a master of Self-energy. At one point in the interview process, the writer, a young gentleman with a bucketload of his own daddy issues, tells Mr. Rogers it must have been hard for his kids to have him as a father. I'm not sure how I would respond if someone told me how hard it must be for my kids to have me as a mother. Probably not awesome.

In this moment, Hanks (playing Rogers) teaches us an incredible lesson about what it looks like to *not* take something personally, even when it has been communicated in an extremely personal way. When the journalist says what he says, it obviously takes Rogers back a bit. But instead of thoughtlessly reacting, he stops talking and stays quiet for a moment. When he speaks again, he thanks the journalist. He tells him he appreciates the perspective. Rogers knew, in that moment, the journalist was likely projecting his own pain into the conversation. He also believed, as noted throughout the film, everyone has a right to their own feelings and feelings are never bad.

Can you imagine how much the social climate in our world would change if we all started to approach conversations more like that? The increase in serenity and compassion would shock the whole system. It would be such a lovely reset button if, for one day, everyone in the world decided to function from the dual mentalities that all things are neutral and nothing is personal. It might shift the social energy of the world on its axis and change our whole psychological trajectory. Wouldn't that be something?

Maybe it's worth a try. The shift starts within each of us. As you strive to curate the life and livelihood you most desire, practice considering that everything is neutral and nothing is personal. See what happens when you start making these changes from the inside in your perceptions and the meanings you assign.

I think about alignment a lot. I seek it out in my physical body. I try to stay well-hydrated, get good sleep, and exercise regularly. I work to keep screen time to a minimum and spend time outdoors as much as possible. I believe in good food, music, thought-provoking conversations, learning opportunities, and nature as medicine. When I'm not feeling like myself, I pay attention and

Alignment

make tweaks accordingly. Every once in a while, it requires the complete removal or replacement of something or someone in my life. Other times, small shifts seem to do the trick. I'm conscious about staying aligned with my values, with my spiritual connection, with the mission for my business, and in my relationships with my kids, husband, family, and friends. Alignment is *everything*. It is the indicator of my access (or lack thereof) to Self-energy. When I feel anything other than myself, I know I'm *out of alignment* in some way.

My niece Lucy and I have mid-September birthdays that fall within five days of each other. We decided that spending a few days sleeping on the ground on the side of a mountain, peeing in the woods, and storing our food in bear-proof containers was the perfect way to celebrate. The first time we went birthday backpack adventuring, we made plenty of rookie mistakes. We let some of the kids bring the full-sized pillows and blankets from their beds, carried our own firewood, and lugged four days' worth of drinking water up the mountain. The adults in the group ended up carrying way more weight on our backs than we should have.

Extra weight and all, we made it up the mountain and had a wonderful few days of exploring, stargazing, hiking, and playing. At the end of our maiden birthday voyage into the wilderness, I was driving a car full of kids back down the mountain. I navigated my way down the curving mountain roads, careful to stay as far as possible from the cliff edge on the right. As I came around a wide curve, the world in front of me suddenly tilted. It was my first-ever experience with vertigo. The feeling reminded me of nights in college when I'd drank too many Jager bombs and wound up laying on my dorm-room bed with one foot on the floor and the opposite hand on the wall in an attempt to get the world to stop spinning.

The feeling was terrifying but, luckily, temporary. I found a spot to pull my car off on the side of the road and waited a few moments while my vision and balance normalized. The task of getting myself and a small gaggle of children safely down the mountain ended up being very slow, careful, and terribly stressful. What I dismissed as dizziness from exhaustion and dehydration happened again a few days later. My husband and I were sitting at our high-top kitchen table having dinner. I was telling Matt about my day when, midsentence, the room tilted in a way that made me feel like we were tiny toys in a dollhouse that someone had capsized. I grabbed the table for support because I thought I was falling and yelped. It scared us both.

The dizzy spells continued to happen every three or four days. Then they started to hit more frequently. I couldn't make sense of why this was happening. Driving a car felt way too risky, so Matt drove me wherever I needed to go for a few days until we could get in to see the doctor. My mind was writing all kinds of horrific worst-case scenario stories. I was certain a brain tumor was growing at an unprecedented speed, threatening to take my life in a matter of days. We set appointments with an ear, nose, and throat (ENT) specialist, my optometrist, and the neurology department. I also scheduled a visit to my chiropractor, Dr. Katie Decker.

When I stepped into her office, it took Dr. Decker about two minutes of poking around to identify that my skull was out of place. Carrying too much weight on my back during the camping trip had pulled the left-side base of my skull away from my vertebrae. The dizzy spells were my body's way of telling me something was very out of alignment.

I can only imagine how big my eyes got when Dr. Decker put on rubber gloves and told me to open my mouth wide. Matt was sitting in a chair against the wall on the other side of the room. My own inner thoughts of "WTF" showed on his face. In all my years working with Dr. Decker, she had never put on rubber gloves. I was freaked. She stuck her finger back between my top and bottom molars on the left side and worked to shift around some little bones behind my gums. Then, she degloved and turned my neck to create a crack loud enough to make all the blood drain from Matt's face. I did not have a brain tumor. And the dizzy spells never happened again.

The vertigo was one symptom stemming from my skeleton being all whacked out, but there had been other issues too. I had been getting headaches and nausea. My right ribs kept popping out of place, which I later learned was because that side of my body was trying to compensate for the goofed-up stuff on my left side. I'd been having a hard time staying focused, I was especially sleepy, and my fear had caused me to stop driving. I was irritable and felt helpless because I didn't know when the next dizzy spell would hit. I so badly wanted to feel like *myself* again. My life, my body, and my mind had become a really crappy place to exist during those few weeks. And it was all because my too-heavy backpack had pulled my damn skull out of place.

Chiropractic care is fascinating to me. It's all about shifting our skeletons back into alignment so the rest of our body can flow and function as it's supposed to. It is incredible how much physical misalignment creates a ripple effect, causing all kinds of troublesome issues. The same is true of personal alignment. When we function within our set of values, stay curious, and remain committed to a sense of purpose, personal alignment is the result. A lack of that kind of functioning results in personal misalignment and causes a ripple effect of hiccups all over the damn place—in our relationships, choices and behaviors, and the way our perceptions are formed. Even our ability to parent clearly, manage finances responsibly, or curate a fulfilling career trajectory can be influenced.

Staying perfectly in alignment all the time and in all ways is an impossible feat for any human. Accidents happen, tragedies strike, we lose jobs, people get sick, and crazy shit goes down in the world. Distress is a normal part of life. So perfection is not the goal. The value of alignment worthy of consistent energy and mindful effort is the process of pursuit rather than the goal of flawlessness. Commit to the quest for alignment, believing the process itself will positively contribute to your level of fulfillment and contentment during this lifetime. It's a fitting example of valuing the journey more than the crossing of some finish line.

Think of the guide for alignment as a clear, thin thread that runs from the day you were born through the moment you take your last breath. It is a fishing line that runs the course of your entire life. It is long, straight, and unbreakable. No knots or tangles. But it's clear and sometimes hard to see, especially when adversity or chaos mucks life up. In some of my darkest times, I've wondered if my line is permanently gone or forever inaccessible.

When we very first start the journey of utilizing introspection and curiosity, the existence of that fishing line may feel like a myth. Crouched on the starting blocks of our journey toward self-actualization is typically the place where we are most out of alignment and feel the least access to Self-energy. It may seem like that guiding thread is so far away we've lost hope of ever finding our way back to it. Take heart. It's there. Our perception of its inaccessibility is only a reflection of our misalignment and the fears of our inner parts. By cracking the door of possibility open, even just enough to peek through with curiosity, you are moving closer to your fishing line already. Keep going. Even if you feel like you're fumbling around in the dark, keep putting one foot in front of the other and stay curious. The line is there. Because *Self* is never gone.

The first migration back to our fishing line is usually the hardest, longest, and most grueling. There will be a thousand moments when you want to give up the hunt for it. If this is where you find yourself right now, look for teeny, tiny ways to touch just one finger to your fishing line. Close your eyes and use your breath, feel your feet on the floor, notice your heart beating, and know you are supported, by your lungs and the ground itself if nothing else. That momentary reassurance, as mild and fleeting as it might be, is a way to locate your line. Remember the eight Cs. Challenge and change anything that blocks you from one or more of them. Because they are what will lead you back into a place of alignment with your*self.*

True alignment is a lot of work. It requires you to place significant amounts of attention and energy on the betterment of your own thoughts, behaviors, choices, and reactions. It demands, in fact, that you place more focus on reconciling and remedying *your own bullshit* than thinking about, talking about, and focusing on other people's bullshit. Once you feel the tremendous amount of risk, discomfort, and energy it takes to leave something as big as a career field, marriage, political conviction, or faith system that does not feel in alignment with your authentic Self, it is unlikely you will ever again stray that far from your fishing line. If you stay awake and aware, you'll never mindlessly trust an untrustworthy person again. You won't answer an invitation with, "Ok, sure, yes," when you know in your guts you want to reply with a giant, "Hell no." Once you know how good it feels to live in alignment, it will take a flight of dragons to pull you too far away from your line ever again.

I have wondered if perhaps a massive tragedy could pull me away from my fishing line. If my husband and children all died, for example, I'm not sure how important alignment would feel to me anymore. I hope I'm wrong about that, but I can understand the "screw it" mentality that could come along with such an epic wound to the soul. I feel like I would eventually desire to feel like myself again. I choose to trust and believe that, even amid astronomical and unimaginable grief and fear, I would set out on the quest to refind my line, even if it had to happen through thousands of tiny baby steps.

If an optimal human experience is important to you, the conviction to forever pursue personal alignment is not just a goal. It is *the* goal. Anything and everything that pulls you very far from your fishing line is, quite frankly, a giant waste of your finite and precious minutes on this planet. Commit, against whatever odds lay ahead of you, to finding your line of alignment. Once you find it, stay tethered to it. Be mindful so you realize when you've started to stray from it as soon as possible. When your course deviates, allow yourself to pause, U-turn, notice, and sincerely wonder how and why the misalignment has happened. Check your integrity and your eight Cs, and use them as a map to get back into alignment as soon and effectively as possible. The line of alignment is where you'll feel most like *yourself*. The flow of all the wonderful things will run most fluidly when you are aligned. Don't wait, start now.

In tight relationship with alignment, *integrity* **is** characterized by a dynamic set of guiding principles. If alignment is an indicator (perhaps *the* indicator) of a felt sense of true *myselfness*, then think of integrity as the bumpers on the sides of the bowling alley lane, holding space and structure so a general sense of alignment is more easily attainable and maintainable. The

Integrity

bumpers can't override free will, and they don't dictate an exact path guaranteeing perfect alignment. Rather, integrity's superpower is one of influential suggestion. It partners with our conscience, trying its darndest to keep us from veering too far off track or into the gutters. Your levels of awareness and commitment to your own integrity will determine how much you do or don't ultimately feel like yourself. When you stay within the bumpers, alignment is attainable. Without clarity and an intentional pledge to your integrity, alignment cannot exist.

Integrity can be defined by two contributing factors. *Both* must be present and work in conjunction for the bumpers of integrity to be intact:

✓ You show up in the world the way you say you want to show up.

✓ You are consistent about it.

That first one requires a legitimate inner consideration about the kind of person you want to be. You can't say one of your core values is kindness but then flip the bird to the guy who cuts you off on the highway. You can't hang your hat on a moral conviction of honesty but then lie to the insurance company, inflating the value of what was stolen from your backseat when your car got broken into. And you are acting as a big, giant fraud if you say you are committed to the spirit of love, forgiveness, and acceptance but then hold grudges, gossip, and harbor judgment in your heart. The first component of integrity requires you take an honest inventory of your own core values and level of active cognitive and behavioral alignments with them.

On a piece of paper, draw one big circle. Make it large enough you can write inside it. But leave enough space around it so you can also write outside the circle. Start to identify thought and behavior patterns and write them either inside or outside the circle. The concepts you include inside your circle will represent thoughts and behaviors that reflect your core values. These are the things that exist *inside* your integrity. Outside the perimeter of your circle, write the thought and behavior patterns that are *not okay with you*. Meanness will likely be written outside your circle, for example. Perhaps kindness is on the inside of your circle. Violence may be on the outside. Maybe compassion is on the inside. Name calling and passive aggressiveness might be written on the outside, while respect might go on the inside of your integrity circle. Be as specific as you can.

You'll notice you often denote one concept on the inside of the circle, then can identify the opposite to be true for the outside. Lying versus honesty, for example. Impatience versus patience.

Cheating versus mutually agreed-upon monogamy.

Self-love versus inner criticism.

Getting drunk versus not getting drunk.

Judgment versus open-mindedness.

Forgiveness versus grudge-holding.

Hate versus love.

If one of your thought patterns or behaviors surfaces and you can't decide where it belongs, sit with that. Rumble with thoughtful consideration until you make peace with which side it belongs on. You may notice some concepts sneak right up against the line with a little bit of blurriness around which side of the fence they fall on. While some things seem as obvious as meanness versus kindness, others aren't so clear. For example, I have a foul mouth. Cursing is part of the passion with which I express myself. It can make vocabulary more colorful and interesting. As far as my own integrity goes, there are few words in the English language that feel more effective, appropriate, or poignant than an intelligently placed f-bomb. This one, for me, lives in a slightly gray area. On my circle chart, it sits close to the line and is dependent on other factors. It is outside of my integrity to use curse words *at* people or fueled in any way by attack or unkindness. Out of respect, I also watch my mouth when communicating with people who feel truly uncomfortable with that kind of language.

Values differ from person to person. This is a normal and totally okay thing. The placement of the things you write on your chart will be dictated by the life you have lived and the ways in which you have been influenced. While having a potty mouth straddles the line of my circle, cursing is marked in clear and certain letters outside of my mom's. It is not part of her integrity.

It is normal for components of this chart to shift over time. It's okay to change your mind as you evolve, get older, and test out different perspectives. Some of the things I felt certain about in my twenties and thirties are things I feel either ambivalent about or quite convicted against now. I'm certain more components of my integrity will transform and alter in the years to come. Shift and change happen when we grow. In fact, I would encourage you to check in with yourself every so often and adjust your circle integrity chart as needed. This would be a fabulous exercise to revisit around the beginning of each new year, especially if you are the kind of person who digs personal reflection and setting New Year's intentions.

The second part of integrity is that in the execution of your values, you remain consistent. This does not mean you have to be perfect. You aren't expected to send the bowling ball straight down the center of the lane, getting an immaculate strike every time. We are all in this same boat of humanness, which, by nature, makes us imperfect and wired for all kinds of struggles and mistake-making. Rather, consistency is the intent and effort to be the same authentic version of yourself regardless of who you are with, what's happening, or what environment you are in. Integrity is the notion that you stay in alignment with your values even when nobody is looking. It's the idea that if you post on social media about the value of being open-minded, you don't turn around and alienate a friend who disagrees with your political views. You can't scold your children for name calling when they are bickering with each other but then refer to the neighbor down the street as an "idiot" when talking to your spouse, even if it's behind closed doors. Integrity is not intact when you lovingly empower and encourage the friends in your life but then allow the shame-based, negative dialogue of inner criticism against yourself.

You cannot claim to live with integrity if you cannot or will not take this kind of personal inventory. If you refuse to do the U-turn and have this important internal conversation with yourself, you will never be clear about the kind of person you want to be. Without that clarity, alignment is nonexistent because there is no defined structure to align with. Life stuckness is often a crisis of unclear integrity. If your mission is to create a life of alignment and authenticity, you can't skip this part of the process. Look inward. Get real. Put it on paper and be honest about it. Then commit.

Back in the day, when our great grandparents talked about *boundaries*, they were referring to property lines or the edge of the garden where the dirt meets the lawn. They weren't having conversations about healthy *personal* boundaries. The term didn't come onto the general public scene until about the 1970s. But now, woah, baby, *boundary* is one of the most obnoxiously overused words in common culture.

Boundaries

Boundaries themselves, true ones, aren't what annoy me. What gets my goat is the abundance with which the term gets thrown around in ways that are used to justify all kinds of dysfunctional behaviors. In this chapter, we'll explore what a personal boundary is. But I think it will be a good use of your time, and mine, to put some focus on what a boundary *isn't*. There's also plenty of banter out there telling us how to establish, communicate, and stay true to our boundaries. That's important stuff. But I don't see many resources floating around telling us how to be better at gracefully receiving and responding to other people's boundaries. So we'll cover that too.

There's a reason this chapter falls in Section 1. With a different twist, it probably could have just as impactfully dropped into Section 2, which is about interpersonal connection. But keep your pants on, we aren't ready for that stuff yet. This conversation belongs right here. Here's why. Boundaries are, first and foremost, an *inside job*. Boundary setting is a method of getting clear about what is okay with us versus what is not okay. (I can't take credit for that simple yet effective definition. I learned it from Brené Brown.) Boundaries are a mechanism of limit setting with intentions around safety and integrity. They are guideposts that define perimeters within various areas of our life meant to hold space for us so we can feel safe, clear, and able to maintain access to Self-energy.

Nobody else can determine what is or isn't okay with you. That discernment is something only *you* can identify and institute. Furthermore, your integrity is a uniquely personal structure that may or may not holistically resonate with others. Your boundaries may very well be influenced by what other people want, think, or expect, but they cannot be determined by or dependent on those things. Your personal boundaries are, most often and primarily, about *you*. So, in support of your authentic *selfness*, your boundaries (even those you create to keep yourself on track) must resonate from a place deep within you.

Personal boundaries are meant to protect and connect. They are necessary and healthy in lots of areas of life. Solid, healthy boundaries will support your physical, emotional, and psychological okayness. They protect your finite time and energy. When we teach kids about physical consent, we guide them in developing safe and healthy boundaries around physical touch, space, and sexual intimacy. Financial boundaries keep us from overborrowing, overloaning, overspending, overgiving, or overhoarding. Whether referring to how people treat you or to the limits around which your teenage daughter is allowed to borrow your favorite pieces from your jewelry box, a good, thoughtful boundary will help protect what feels healthy, safe, and important.

Here's where things get twisted. I hear people throw around the term "boundaries" as if they are ironclad, steel-plated, bulletproof, welded-shut doors. "So-and-so said something that hurt my feelings, so my boundary is I will never say hello or make eye contact with them ever again." Or, "That monster molested a child and deserves to be locked away in solitary confinement until they die." Those are not boundaries, people. Those are walls. They are division. They are rooted in fear and insecurity. People who use the tactics of minimization, justification, violence, blame, judgment, grudge holding, abuse, or disrespectful behavior are scared to death to wrestle with their own dysfunction, their blind spots, or the scary possibilities that don't match their desired outcomes. Those who lack the willingness to truly open their minds and hearts to perspectives other than their own are not setting boundaries. They are avoiding. They are deflecting. What they mislabel as "boundaries" is actually their best attempts to protect themselves by trying to control and manipulate the situation. Pushing others away is the quickest and most convenient attempt to maladaptively dodge or discharge one's own anxiety and discomfort.

True boundaries are more like a screen door. There's an option to lock it, and the glass slider can be lowered when the weather is just a little too chilly to let the outdoor breeze flow into the house. But it doesn't create complete division. There's opportunity and the possibility for exchange and cooperation, as long as both parties are willing and able to function in a state of mutual understanding, empathy, and respect. Contrary to too many misinformed assumptions, healthy boundaries are not necessarily created to divide or separate people. Rather, true boundaries can be a conduit for better connection and possible healing through deeper levels of understanding.

This is not to say there aren't appropriate times to disconnect or permanently turn the page on a situation, phase of life, or relationship. If an individual vengefully murders people, of course it is an appropriate boundary to remove that person from free society and place them somewhere secure, where both they and others can be kept safe. When a teenager lies to his parents about where he spent the previous night and they find out he used dangerous drugs and put himself in sketchy situations, temporarily taking away all privileges to be in unsupervised social settings might be a fair boundary. The screen door, however, leaves room for the belief that people deserve to be heard and cared for, even in their most dysfunctional moments. The glass slider can be lifted so evolution and better understanding can stand a chance. This perspective on boundaries relies on the faith that people have the potential to make better choices and heal. Or, at a minimum, that they deserve humanistic care, safety, and some level of positive regard.

There's a difference between boundaries and barriers. The ironclad, welded-shut door is a barrier. It says, "I'm right;

you're wrong; get out of my face." It leaves no room for curiosity. No room for even a sliver of light to shine through with the possibility of connection. This kind of approach is the work of our most protective and defensive parts. Not Self. Barriers involve a refusal to consider another person as a human with value deserving respect or (at a minimum) common decency. Close-mindedness to those fundamental truths is an attempt to create disconnection, obtain power, or prove a point. A person who can stand in their integrity while also extending respect and curiosity (especially after being hurt or in conflict) is a person with stellar access to Self-energy. Because Self is inherently confident, it doesn't need power. It doesn't need to prove a point. Self understands every human has value and the right to their opinions and perspectives. Self believes people make mistakes, sometimes horrific ones, yet still are deserving of love.

Self also understands the value of forgiveness and knows how to harness the concept of *bless and release.* The screen door has a lock for a reason. Sometimes situations do require we cut ties and walk away. However, the lock doesn't take away the visibility through the glass. Walking away doesn't give us the right to forget the humanness of others. It's okay to boldly say "NO." It's okay to draw a line in the sand. But don't do it out of contempt or resentment. Spite-motivated actions are a barrier, a door slammed in the face of others. An endgame boundary may truly be appropriate when it is time to take some space or say goodbye, not with unkindness or disrespect and not to prove a point, but because it is sincerely the most loving thing for everyone involved.

Now let's turn the table and put ourselves on the receiving end of someone else's boundaries. This is where I'd love to swerve the topic and bypass the part where we get real vulnerable and vulnerably real. I am the very first to raise my hand and admit how much I struggle with this. Some strong emotions and my defensive parts make accepting the boundaries of others one of the biggest challenges of my life. I'm a work in progress too, people. In order to move forward together, let's fall back on one of the oldest morality roadmaps in the book: do unto others as you'd have them do unto you. If you want to be heard and respected when something feels crummy to you, you've gotta be willing to do the same for others.

When we look inward and get clear on something that does not feel okay to us and then gather the courage to speak up for it, our hope can't be that others will ultimately understand or agree with us. I mean, that would be awesome. But in moments when we have to speak up about a personal boundary, that's rarely the case. Rather, our hope is they will attempt to consider our perspective, believe our intentions are loving, trust we are doing the best we can, and respect the boundary we are communicating regardless of whether or not they understand or agree with it. Or, in the worst best-case scenario, if they don't understand or agree with our boundary, the hope is they will choose to believe our intentions are good, honor our personal differences, and step away from the situation or relationship in a mature and respectful way.

We can't expect from others what we won't hold ourselves accountable to. It's as simple as that. I was punched straight in the nose by this hard lesson years ago through my best friend. Rooney had made plans to travel to Colorado for a three-day camping weekend with me and one of our other girlfriends. The timing of this trip was purposeful. All three of us desperately needed a break from the transitions, turmoil, and chaos of our lives. This quick weekend getaway was meant to be a healing reset for all three of us. We had planned to adventure in nature, hike, laugh, eat one thousand s'mores, and enjoy each other's company. It was meant to be a rejuvenating pause.

This was during the years when my now-husband and I were dating long-distance. Matt and I hadn't seen each other in more than a month, but he knew about my camping plans with the girls and was supportive. About a week before the trip, I was flailing in an attempt to keep my head above water and having some especially hard days. I was trying to finish grad school while working full-time at an internship position and part time as a fitness instructor. The single-mom thing was kicking my ass. And my dad's health was rapidly declining, which meant my mom often needed my support and help. I was fried, completely exhausted, and emotionally spent. And while I truly did want to see my girlfriends and I knew the mountain air would feel good, all I really wanted was to be snuggled up in my boyfriend's arms with zero responsibilities so I could cry and sleep as much as I needed to. I was desperately craving someone to take care of me.

I called Rooney and told her I'd changed my mind. I bailed on our camping trip and had booked a flight to Kansas to see Matt instead. In true Rooney fashion, she said, "Okay," and didn't argue.

Two weeks later, Rooney texted and asked if we could talk. She had taken the time to U-turn inward and be curious about what she was feeling and why. She explained that she'd felt disappointed and upset about my abrupt decision to bail on our camping plans. While she understood how I felt and respected my decision to do what felt best to me, she explained it had resulted in some hurt feelings and anger. She and our other friend had changed their schedules and arrangements in order to make travel and our camping trip possible. Rooney explained she felt disrespected by my actions. She communicated a new hesitancy to make those kinds of plans with me. And, because she'd made the effort to be introspectively curious and get clear about what she needed in the future, Rooney was able to share her newly formed personal boundary. She explained if we were going to make plans that required her to travel, make childcare arrangements, miss work, be away from her family, or cost her money, she'd appreciate it if I erred on the side of saying, "No," or, "Maybe," instead of "Yes," at least until I felt a greater sense of stability under my feet.

My defensive and explainer parts wanted to talk my way out of this tense spot and make her understand why I'd made the choice to bail on our camping plans. My point-proving parts were dying for her to have compassion for my pain. The problem was, while I knew she wasn't going to do happy cartwheels about my decision to ditch on them, I'd hoped she would perceive my feelings as more important than her own. I had acted selfishly. I'd made a decision that significantly affected other people without using curiosity in an attempt to understand how my choice had landed with my friends or to consider alternative options that included the girls. Her newly communicated personal boundary, as Rooney explained it, would help protect her heart from future disappointment and hurt feelings while also minimizing the risk she'd feel resentful toward me. This limit was her way of doing the most loving thing for herself, me, and our friendship.

Because she was courageous enough to talk to me about her feelings, Rooney and I were able to more deeply know and understand each other. And because she made the conscious effort to get clear about what felt crappy and what would feel better in the future, we were able to lay the groundwork for more fair and appropriate expectations moving forward. My role was to set my own defensive cravings aside, open my heart and my ears, and intentionally try to understand her more fully. Accessing empathy required I lay down my own ego. Together, Rooney and I treated the situation as a screen door, an opportunity for healing and greater connection. Her willingness to bravely create and respectfully communicate a boundary, combined with my willingness to receive and respect it, laid the tracks for a more bonded friendship. It was scary and vulnerable for us both but resulted in truckloads of benefit. Since that day, we've not once found ourselves in conflict gridlock with each other. We now know the value of having solid personal boundaries and communicating them to each other, and we are both willing and capable of gracefully being on the receiving end of those limit-setting conversations.

Whether we're talking about two or more individuals or giant groups of people, personal boundaries are imperative to connection and healing. This is true in romantic relationships, work environments, political parties, communities, families, and friendships. Communicating our own boundaries to others is hard. It is arguably *impossible* if we don't first pause to go inward with a curiosity-infused U-turn. Once we have greater clarity on what we are feeling, what we are thinking, and what we need to be different and we feel emotionally and behaviorally self-regulated, *then* we are prepared to go to another person or group of people and bravely share how things can be better moving forward.

Interestingly, introspection and curiosity are also the first orders of business when you catch yourself on the receiving end of someone else's communicated personal boundary. When someone comes to you with their boundary, pause in humility and stay out of reactivity. Dial inward and discover which of your protective parts might be firing up. Tend to those before responding. Call on courage, stay within your integrity, and proceed with a learner's mind. Believe that it ultimately behooves you to prioritize clarity, empathy, and connection over your need to be *right*. After all, boundaries are not about winning. They are about advocating for yourself and the pursuit of connection.

You can tell a lot about how much turmoil a person has lived through by their bandwidth for distress. Surviving hardships creates resilience. Life struggles serve as an expander, growing an individual's ability to persevere through hard things, our *window of tolerance*.

When distress pushes the boundaries of your current window of tolerance, you are faced with a choice.

Window of Tolerance

You can crumble and surrender to a woe-is-me mentality. You can react, blaming or lashing out against others. Or you can call on courage and curiosity and look inward, feeling your way through the tunnel of discomfort, stretching the limits of what you think you can handle.

I have observed this dynamic firsthand with young people in my community. In my career as a psychotherapist, I often work with teenagers, so I'm on the front lines of suicidality in our high schools. According to the National Institute of Mental Health, the rate of suicide in the United States has been on a steady upward tick since the early 2000s. Right here in the Denver, Colorado area, there is an interesting observable difference in adolescent suicidality when comparing inner-city schools, which have students from lower average household incomes, to the schools where the average household income is significantly higher.

A few years ago, I worked as a group facilitator for a local nonprofit organization, leading a team of teens interested in advocating for and serving their local teenage peers in some sort of struggle. My team chose to target mental health issues. The kids and I worked together, researching and interviewing people on the topic. We found that the interviewed teenage population of kids who had lived through ongoing turmoil and adversity had, on average, significantly higher abilities to handle new adversity. In other words, they had a relatively large window of tolerance. By contrast, the interviewed teens who had experienced lower levels of economic and general life struggle tended to have a lower level of distress tolerance.

The kids from the less-privileged schools would tell us stories about how they were being raised by a single mom, for example, and were helping to make sure their younger siblings were fed and put to bed at night. They would tell us about times when they'd heard gunshots outside their bedroom windows at night, or days when they didn't have money to keep the electricity on or replace their shoes when their toes burst out the front of their sneakers. When we asked these high schoolers how much distress they felt when they missed out on a social event or when they'd been rejected by a group of peers, they mostly shrugged it off and said they had lived through much worse. They reported feeling confident in their ability to be okay, even when bad things happen.

Contrary to that schema of resilience, we noticed the distress tolerance of the teens from suburban, higher-income households who had experienced, on average, significantly less financial and basic safety-related adversity struggled to believe they could handle hard things. When asked to identify one of the most distressing things they could imagine, many of these kids answered that having their iPhones taken away as a form of discipline was at the top of their list. They described experiences of being broken up with, left out of a social gathering, or rejected by peers as if they were the worst things they could imagine and perhaps worthy of suicidal considerations.

The teens who had experienced less life adversity (particularly related to health, safety, or finances) had not, on average, yet been given quite as intense of opportunities to realize how very equipped they actually were to move through difficult situations, events, and emotions. In reality, one teen is not intrinsically more capable of surviving adversity than another. Rather, each kid's *perception* of how much they can handle is different. Those who had lived through more threats to health, stability, and safety (of themselves or people they loved) had been blessed, in a weird way, with lessons that had highlighted their ability to persevere. Whereas those who had lived through less real or perceived risk to livelihood, safety, and the ability to thrive simply didn't *believe* they could handle hard experiences and emotions.

To understand the concept of the window of tolerance, think of yourself as Pac-Man. And let's pretend every little pellet is a difficult moment or situation in life. Every pellet, while perhaps tasting awful and being hard to swallow, will grow Pac-Man's window of tolerance and teach him important things. Pac-Man will grow bigger with every pellet he eats. Before you know it, Pac-Man has grown so big and strong the pellets have become much less intimidating. He still doesn't necessarily like to eat them because, well, they taste like crap. But he's not so afraid of them anymore. He doesn't freak out when a pellet is in his path. He knows he can call upon all the resilience and wisdom he's gained from past pellet eating and, if he must, get the next one down his gullet too. Pac-Man understands his window of tolerance for distress is dynamic, stretchable, and capable of expanding.

To *tolerate* means to allow the existence, occurrence, or practice of something we don't necessarily like or agree with. It means to accept or endure. Bad things happen. Sometimes the bad things could have been avoided. Other times they are fluke happenstance misfortunes. It doesn't matter which is which. What matters is the meaning we assign to the stressful events and lessons we learn from them. Every adversity has gifts for us if we are willing to receive them. Every hard thing you've experienced in life has educated you on something about yourself, someone else, or the world around you. Every pain we feel has a flip side. Every failure offers something important to learn.

We can handle a great deal more adversity than we give ourselves credit for. Every time I sit in my therapist chair and listen to a story about how someone has overcome incredible odds or survived a horrendous trauma, I am reminded of how insanely resilient the human spirit is. Adverse life lessons and experiences, however, are not without their remnant burdens. With every new wound, we receive a new scar, a stone cast into the path of our naturally flowing curiosity. We learn to be afraid of pain. We find that trust can be dangerous. We realize how precarious love can be. And we come to know that vulnerability is never, ever without risk.

In a dream world, curiosity would flow uninterrupted. We would provide and receive steady streams of it with every exchange of information. But the more years we live in this world and the more life we experience, inertia and resistance increase both inside and outside of us, blocking the natural flow of curiosity. In any flow of water, the force of gravity draws the water current from higher elevations down toward the lower elevations. But when enough rocks, stones, and boulders get piled up in the path of the flow, even the strong Colorado rivers, with their spring-snow runoff, can get backed up. If we allow them to, difficult life experiences can strangle curiosity.

Our own personal struggles and painful life experiences aren't the only things that back up the flow of curiosity. From the day we are born, we are taught that discomfort is bad. There is an entire segment of the human emotional experience that media tries to convince us is avoidable. Coca-Cola has said when you crack a bottle of soda, you "open happiness" (because apparently sadness is a terribly unattractive emotion to feel). Visiting the "happiest place on Earth" tugs at Disney tourists' hope to escape monotony or boredom. Every ad for psychopharmaceuticals tries to convince you their magic pill will solve your feelings of anxiety, depression, or mood swings. More often than not, when someone is trying to sell you something, they are banking on the assumption you have aversions to negative emotions.

I wonder what would happen if we stopped hating on the less comfortable emotions? What if we quit labeling hard feelings as *bad*? What might it feel like to make room for *all* our emotions? Is it possible our resilience might grow from this uncomfortable practice? You betcha. In fact, I would dare say the potential for growth *only* exists in places of discomfort, which means *welcoming* distress is actually an invitation for personal evolution.

When my stepdaughter Brekhan was ten years old, we started working with an orthodontist to get her teeth aligned and straight. At that age, she had some grown-up teeth that still needed to drop in. There was some crowding preventing that process from happening, so the first step was to install an expander. A device was placed in the roof of her mouth to hold the arch of her top teeth in a nice wide curve. For the first thirty days, we adjusted the device so it slowly and subtly pushed her teeth into a slightly wider formation, making room for the remaining adult teeth to drop down into the right places. Every night before bedtime, we'd take a tiny, little, metal key that fit into a hole in the center of the expander. We would crank the key one time from front to back, moving the contraption in such a way it would gently press from the inside of her teeth to create a teeny bit more width in the curve. Then we'd send her to bed before the soreness kicked in. It was a slobber-filled, achy month for Brekhan, but it did the trick beautifully! Think of curiosity as that expander. When we use it, discomfort is the price we pay for making room for new perspectives and experiences and growing our window of tolerance for adversity.

I'm a recovering control freak. I relapse pretty much on the daily but have come a humongously long way from my OCD-esque addictions of the past. One of those attachments was to my hard-copy, handwritten day planner. I lived, slept, and breathed according to that thing. It was organized and color coded to the hilt. I hand wrote every commitment, reminder, work shift, and coffee date onto those pages. If I went to a movie with friends, I wrote down the name of the movie, the time, the theater location, and who I was going with. Then I'd highlight it in hot pink because that was my "fun social things" category. There was something about handwriting all the details of my life into this planner that felt satisfying and safe to me.

During my undergraduate work, I would write every assignment and responsibility into my planner. I would feel a great sense of accomplishment when I could cross through each one with my black, fine-tipped sharpie, denoting I had completed that task. I was super late to the technology game when the iPhones came out, with all its fancy iCloud synchronization capabilities, including a digital calendar that would flow between your computer and your phone. I remember learning you could color code calendar appointments and thinking, "Look at them trying to be a day planner; that's so cute." But no thank you; it wasn't for me. I didn't trust a device to securely hold information nor to respond to my needs at the same level of efficiency that pen on paper and my collection of colorful Sharpies and highlighters could.

At some point, my job started requiring me to use a digital calendar. So for a while, I was doing both. I would hand write everything into my day planner, then follow up by also adding it to the computer so my colleagues could see my availability and whereabouts. The double-documenting ordeal was a racket. But the distress I felt inside myself whenever I considered converting wholly over to the digital calendar was real. If you are not the same in this regard, this example probably won't resonate with you. But if you know, you know! My fellow control junkies, do you feel me?!

On the first day I finally worked up enough curiosity and courage to leave my day planner at home, I cried. Not even kidding. I felt so stressed, uncomfortable, and out of sorts. Logically, I knew I wasn't going to die. But I was pretty sure I might forget every commitment and to-do item scheduled for that day. As it turned out, the digital system worked better than I anticipated, and I eventually adapted, ditching the hard-copy planner altogether. Ultimately, the transition was incredibly helpful and (I say this with a sense of defeat but sincerity) *more* efficient and effective than my day planner. The increase in discomfort was an unavoidable part of the process.

I'm being a bit dramatic with the day-planner example. The discomfort was legitimate. But that's a fairly chill, somewhat mundane example of window-of-tolerance expansion. Then there are times when curiosity leads us to really scary places, much more so than the ache of transitioning away from my day planner. These are the moments when the lightbulb comes on in your head and you clearly realize, "Yes, *this* is the way. This is my truth." Then, the very next thought that enters your mind is, "Oh shit!"

These are the forks in the road. We all have dozens and dozens of them throughout the course of our lives. These are the times when we look in one direction and are tempted by the paths of avoidance, justification, minimization, deflection, excuse making, blame, "Yeah, buts," or outright denial. That is the path of familiarity and comfort.

Then we glance in the new direction (the one that evoked the "Oh shit" response), and we feel the pangs of fear, uncertainty, guaranteed discomfort, and, at worst, outright pain. These are divine opportunities to expand our windows of tolerance. They are the linchpin moments of life when we are called to be courageous and trust that the painful experience of stretching the limits of what we think we can handle will ultimately be worth it. Leaving my first marriage was one of those.

My marriage to Sean was built on a very cracked foundation. He and I met in our midtwenties, partied together, and had a ton of fun being young and ornery. He proposed eleven months after we met; we got married five months after that. It was a whirlwind. We barely knew ourselves at all. Neither Sean nor I had even begun the individual process of self-exploration. I doubt either of us could have explained what the word *introspection* even meant back then. We were both bullheaded and naïve, which is a destructive combination. Trauma in relationships had touched both of our lives. But we had no idea how much those prior experiences had affected either of us. Our relationship was a tug of war between deeply loving each other and truly wanting to build an incredible life together, and being stuck in our own individual spirals of dysfunction that we hadn't even begun to look critically at yet. It was like trying to weave together the threads of a friendship bracelet without having the other end tethered to anything. We were attempting to build a life and grow a marriage together while the relationship unraveled from the other end.

After a two-month separation just one year into the marriage, a pregnancy soon after, and baby number two arriving a few years later, the foundation of our relationship was still no stronger than it was when we started. We tried to convince ourselves this surface-level marital coexistence was normal and healthy. But somewhere down in my soul, I believed marriage could be more, could be deeper. We were seven years in, and I had completely forgotten who I was aside from the beautiful, storybook life we pretended to be living. It was the furthest thing from an authentic existence. For years, I sat and cried alone in the back of the bedroom closet, wondering why I was so unhappy. I poured my thoughts and heart out in letters to Sean and conversations with him. But he struggled with parts of himself that wanted to deny and minimize the issues. He wanted desperately to believe everything was okay. He didn't want to look under the surface at his own brokenness any more than I wanted to look at mine.

By June 2012, almost exactly seven years into our marriage, I was multiple months into my first-ever deep-dive therapeutic journey. I was, for the first time in my life, using curiosity to truly get to know my truest self. More and more with each passing week, I began to have faith that I was equipped to stretch the limits of my comfort and familiarity. I had a keen awareness of the need to expand my window of tolerance and knew, with my whole heart, that it was the only way to find freedom and peace. That month, I left Sean home in Colorado with our four-year-old daughter and one-year-old son to attend a friend's wedding back in my home state of Kansas. Then I flew directly to Texas for a few days of work at my company's annual convention. Those days away gave me the space and stillness to be curious. Sitting alone in my hotel room, I noticed what it felt like to be without Sean, to sleep in a bed alone, to rely on my own abilities, and to function autonomously.

As unfamiliar and truly uncomfortable as it was, I noticed I felt more like myself. That made me more curious, and I started to consider what I wanted marriage to *feel* like (not just *look* like to everyone on the outside). Healthy marriage had never been modeled for me, so I had no reference for the measurement of *good*, much less *thriving*. I wasn't totally sure what I wanted or was looking for. But I felt an enormous amount of clarity that what my soul craved was *not this*. I intuitively knew I was built for something deeper. Something more inspiring and connective, more raw, more real.

After more than a year of wrestling with the thought, the lightbulb in my head came on, and the truth was crystal clear. In the pursuit to feel like myself again, I realized I could not stay in the marriage. It wasn't sustainable. It was blocking and disallowing my authenticity, which I knew would result in me turning into a bitter, resentful, and unhappy wife and mother. I didn't want to do that to Sean, our kids, or myself. I remember sitting on the edge of the bed in my hotel room with my head in my hands thinking, "Shit. Shit, shit, shit, shit, shit." I had uncovered the undeniable truth of what needed to happen. But it meant I was heading straight into massive amounts of long-term discomfort, inconvenience, and tremendous pain for myself, Sean, our families, and our children.

When my work trip was over, I flew home to Denver, silent tears streaming down my face for the entirety of the flight. When I got home, the kids were at daycare, and Sean was sitting in our home office, working on his computer. I didn't even take my suitcase up to the bedroom. I walked in and asked him if we could talk.

I made sure to look him in the eye and say, as gently as possible, "I want a divorce, and I'm so sorry." The whole of the situation was so much more complicated than that. But by this point, everything else had been said dozens of times before to no avail. These were the only words left to say.

He said, "Okay," then walked upstairs. A few minutes later, I followed him up there and found Sean sitting silently on our bed with his back against the tall, black headboard. I felt like my heart was being cut out of my body. I fought the urge to vomit. Neither of us could speak. We both knew it was over.

I loved Sean with my whole heart. I wanted so badly for my life-long partner to be him. For the eight years since I'd met him, I had loved him more than I had loved myself. Rather than standing firm in healthy boundaries and my own authenticity, I had rationalized all the issues in our relationship. I didn't want to hurt him or the kids, and I was afraid of being alone. My own pain and suffering from the wounds of my past were bleeding out all over this man I loved. I was projecting my bottomless desire to be deeply known and loved onto a person who wasn't equipped or healthy enough to offer those things. I made it his responsibility to fix my pain, which was not fair. To make matters worse, I was stuck in a pattern of being hurt by Sean's own repetitive cycles of dysfunction, reacting with my own dysfunction, then codependently brushing it all under the rug so we could get back to "normal" as quickly as possible. Then we'd naively cross our fingers and say some prayers, hoping it would be the last time the bad things happened.

Meanwhile, my own self-identity was being chipped away at. I barely recognized myself anymore. I walked with my head down. I spoke with an insecure voice. I second-guessed myself constantly. My creativity was gone. Weirdly, my eyes didn't even look the same brightness of blue they once had. I felt like such a watered-down version of myself. If I had stayed, I fear there would have eventually come a day when my authenticity was buried too deeply to ever recover. Curious introspection reminded me that my *Self* was still in there and deserved to be advocated for. The willingness to U-turn inward toward my intuition, a spirit of hope, and a faith in something bigger than us was exactly the introspective energy needed to make this pivotal decision and get my life trajectory back on its tracks and into alignment. Familiarity, comfort, and (what I perceived to be) certainty would have kept me stuck and sad, likely for the rest of my life. Curiosity saved me. But it started by excruciatingly expanding my window of tolerance. My choice to leave the marriage led us both straight into the worst day and year of our lives.

To this day, I still love Sean, a lot. But now I also love *myself*. While curiosity started me down the trailhead of all that pain, that same exact hike has led me to a happiness with myself and a freedom-filled existence I didn't previously know was possible. The undoing had to be done. I remember feeling so fascinated by the curiosity-led epiphany that the foundation of marriage is *not* the relationship with each other. Rather, the fertile ground for a partnership to bond, grow, root down, and rise up comes first from the inner work and *both* individuals' conviction to establish and maintain a healthy and secure *sense of Self*. Commitment to each other is secondary to that. It *has* to be. I grew up being shown and taught that the only way to have a lasting marriage was death to the Self for the sake of the partnership. I had been led astray, misinformed. A successful marriage is a union in which each individual has a secure and healthy sense of Self working in conjunction with a mutual decision to do life in tandem, encouraging and empowering each other's authenticity. It's the opposite of believing that Self should die.

A joy-filled, authentic existence was the desired outcome for me, so the deconstruction process was unavoidable. The only way to get past the pain was to walk straight into and all the way through it. I learned through that experience how strong I could be, how much discomfort I could tolerate. I now know that I can do *really* hard things. I will never again believe I need to play small in order to be okay. That tsunami-level storm taunted me with a thousand reasons why I couldn't do it, how I'd never make it. And in response, I looked that storm straight in the eye and told it, "*Watch me.*"

If we believe our window of tolerance for discomfort and pain is minimal, we will choose the path of familiarity. We will stay meager, make excuses, play the victim, blame others, and believe the lie that we are safe. When curiosity knocks on our door and we walk outside to see a twenty-thousand-foot mountain ahead of us full of difficult terrain and unpredictable weather, it is easier to turn around, walk back inside, shut the door, and tell curiosity, "No thanks, buddy. Not today." But when we remember we are equipped with everything we need to make that unfamiliar and difficult climb and tap into our deep reservoir of courage, we take the first step...then the next...then the next. With every bump and bruise, we grow. We learn. We become more resilient as our window of tolerance expands. And every new scar becomes a landmark of our journey, documentation of the good fight in the name of authenticity.

The best part of this whole thing is the understanding that we don't have to be afraid of the future. Every time the pain expands us, we prepare and equip ourselves even better for the future struggles ahead of us. Insecurities and fearful thoughts shrink into background whispers as our resilience grows bigger and wider. And we no longer feel the need to predict the storms. We are hardwired for struggle from the day we step into this world. Mistakes, pain, and failure are guaranteed. So instead of living in fear of those future struggles, we can relax, stay in the flow of curiosity, and know we will be able to handle it all when the next storm hits. We can embrace the pursuit to expand our window of tolerance for distress, knowing it will serve us well as we move forward, toward, and through the toughest terrain of this life.

Section 2

Connection with Others

So far, Section 1 has equipped you with stronger introspection and curiosity muscles when it comes to looking within, understanding yourself more fully, and shifting your thoughts and actions into better alignment with your integrity. In a nutshell, Section 1 was all about helping you realize a more authentic version of yourself. In and of itself, that's pretty rewarding and feels much better. But we aren't stopping there. Improved connection to yourself is just the beginning. Now, we step into the pursuit of healthier and more meaningful relationships with other people. This second section is all about *interpersonal connection.*

There is an unspoken agreement that when we engage with another person (a new friend, romantic partner, business colleague, or neighbor), we are willingly stepping into a spotlight of exposure. There is an expectation that both individuals plan to open up, contribute some level of vulnerable energy, and are willing to be known and seen by someone else.

From an IFS parts perspective, entering into a relationship with another person is like attending a joint family reunion. You and all your inner system parts are showing up for your own party while agreeing to overlap and intersect with the other person's circus of parts. Every time one of your "family members" (parts) meets one of theirs, there's an unavoidable tango. Each new character (part) comes with its own unique personality, varying perspectives, intentions and agendas, fears, motives, and life experiences. When coming into contact, some interpersonal parts will jive with each other nicely. Others, not so much. One or more of their parts may trigger the shit out of one or more of yours and vice versa. Considering each of us has hundreds of protective parts on constant lookout for things that can hurt or offend us, attempting to do relationships with other humans can result in one hell of a parts party. No wonder relationships are so hard!

With that kind of chaos and complexity, why would anyone want to be in relationships with other people? (The introverted parts of me are nodding in agreement and would love nothing more than to go all *Into the Wild* and run away to an isolated cabin in the mountains.) The answer is simple: we are hardwired for connection. Humans are built to do life together. We are biologically, neurologically, and psychologically set up to bond, mate, laugh, create, grieve, love, work, raise children, and do community *together*. Not alone. And (much to the dismay of my introverted parts) relationships with other people can be *awesome*.

Many of the best moments in life feel incredible because they are shared with others.

This potential for relational amazingness increases exponentially when two or more people have sincere intentions for connective reciprocity. If both sides are willing to utilize skills such as active listening, authentic question asking, perspective taking, and empathy, interpersonal connection becomes fluid and deeply bonding. Our deepest fears and protective responses to pain and uncertainty cause our parts to keep our swords and shields up and active. But curiosity empowers us to set our weapons down and move in closer to each other. It emboldens us with courage to risk ending up in pain and disappointment in exchange for the possibility that we might gain friendship, collaboration, and love.

Through curiosity and empathy, deep, meaningful relationships are formed. Communities come together, important change is created, and nations are healed. I recognize this might sound like a pie-in-the-sky perspective. That's fine; maybe it is. But I've seen it happen with my own two eyes, so I refuse to be anything other than a believer. In both my business and personal lives, I have felt the benefits of making interpersonal connections this way. It has been nothing short of life-changing and life-giving.

I can't promise this pursuit will be without discomfort, or even that your brave and vulnerable efforts will be kindly received every time. But I can tell you, with all the sincerity in my heart, that you will experience a radically positive shift within yourself and your relationships with people who are equally as invested in meaningful interpersonal connection.

It's not easy, but it's not rocket science either. As we remember our own personal humanity and then do others the same solid, we feel better. We've already read up on how to feel more like *ourselves*. In this section, we'll learn how to hold curious space and give others the permission to feel and function more like *themselves*. That's when painful wounds begin to heal and all the best kinds of relational magic start to happen.

Interpersonal connection can be the most incredible medicine and conduit for joy. It can also be a psychological roller coaster. Buckle up.

Imagine you carry an invisible backpack at all times. We all do. In this backpack, you carry bricks. Lots of them. These bricks are different sizes and weights. Etched into each one is the burden it represents. One person may carry a brick that says, "I was sexually abused when I was ten years old." Another person may be carting around the weight of a brick that says, "I'm gay, and I am afraid to tell my parents."

Bricks + Backpacks

Perhaps you or someone you know hauls around bricks of, "I've had three miscarriages," "I went through a divorce five years ago," "My dad has never once said he's proud of me," "I hate my body," "My wife is having an affair," "I had an abortion when I was nineteen years old", "I struggle with anxiety," "I have learning differences," or "I just found out I have cancer." These would all be terribly heavy bricks.

Among our most heavy and burdensome bricks are a compilation of smaller ones. For example, "I didn't sleep well last night," is a brick I carry around on some days. "I have one hundred hours of responsibilities this week but only half that time to actually tend to them," might be one of yours. "My sinuses are congested, and I don't physically feel quite like myself today," "The weather is cold and gloomy," or "Tomorrow is my first day back to work after vacation, and I don't want to go," are all examples of bricks that aren't life-altering, but they can absolutely weigh us down, especially when they pile up.

Nobody is immune or exempt from the burdensome weight of the bricks in our backpacks. It does not matter how charmed one's life may be, the bricks are there, and the backpack can be heavy. In the spirit of curiosity, it is critical you are able and willing to look inward often and explore the inventory of bricks you carry around in your backpack. *Know your bricks.* Even the smaller ones. And be willing to consider there are likely some bricks tucked away in the deepest hidden pockets of your backpack you haven't even identified yet.

Beyond the awareness of your own heavy backpack and its contents, the next important concept to understand and consider is the *exchange* of bricks between people. This is where things get real interesting.

I had a friend years ago who put a post on Facebook sharing a photo of herself in a cocktail dress. Underneath, she included a caption that read, "Went shopping today, and I'm soooo in love with my cute, new, little black dress...ugh, now if only I could just lose another ten pounds so I could look good in it!"

It doesn't require much genius to sense what is happening here. This gal was fishing. In essence, she reached into her backpack; took hold of the brick that said, "Body insecurities;" and held it out for her Facebook network to tend to.

You can guess the kinds of responses she received in the comments section. "Oh girl, you're so beautiful!" "You don't need to lose weight, you look amazing!" "I'd give anything to have your figure, the dress looks fabulous!" By replying in this way, these respondents were communicating, "Oh gosh, that body-image brick looks heavy, let me take that and fix it for you."

Let me be clear: there is a time and place for helping people when they are overburdened by their bricks. More on that in a minute. But it is *not* okay for others to function under the general expectation that you will carry or fix their bricks *for* them. Nor is it okay for you to hand your bricks over to others with that same kind of assumption.

For example, if you have daddy issues, first of all, welcome to the club. Also, don't hand that shit over to the men in your life, expecting them to fix those wounds for you. That's not cool. Trust me, I've done it. It's terribly unhealthy and not a sustainable solution. When we look to another person, group of people, situation, achievement, or particular outcome to fill the holes left by the wounds of our past, we receive (at best) a synthetic and temporary solution to the pain. A Band-Aid. To make matters worse, this approach usually ends up delaying our own attention to our internal struggles and the pursuit of wholehearted healing. It trains us to depend on external redeemers to ease the pain.

When you hold grudges against, bad-mouth, or hold in negative regard another person, you scream, "I have insecurity bricks." These behaviors are examples of more ego-based protective mechanisms that attempt to discharge the pain and discomfort of your self-worth issues. It is a terrible thing to want someone else to fail or feel badly. That dysfunctional allocation of insecurity bricks makes you small. It diminishes your light and mucks up your energy. That's no good for anyone—*you* in particular.

It can also be incredibly damaging and unhealthy to take on other people's bricks. You already carry enough of your own. The weight becomes debilitating if you start adding the heaviness of other people's bricks to your own backpack. Thanks to my own overfunctioning caretaking and people-pleasing parts, I have firsthand knowledge of the heaviness that comes from chronically taking on other people's bricks. Helloooooooo, codependency! That kind of behavior enables the dysfunction of the brick-hander-over-er while simultaneously sucking the finite energy resources right out of your own mind, body, and spirit. It leads to burnout and fatigue. Those of us with codependent parts who believe it's up to us to keep everyone else safe, happy, calm, and comfortable know what it feels like to be running on fumes while forgetting where we end and others begin. It creates a dynamic similar to the car that never stops to refuel. Eventually it breaks down and stops running.

Okay now, let's not be totally insensitive. Of course there are times in life when it is honorable and loving to walk alongside other people and help carry their bricks when their own backpacks have become extraordinarily heavy. Let's say you have a neighbor lady who has two dogs, a pretty flower garden, and a strong aversion to cooking. One morning, you wake up to a text informing you that this lady's husband died in his sleep last night. It might be very appropriate for you to offer to take care of her dogs, water her garden, and provide a few meals over the upcoming weeks as she grieves and adjusts to life after this tragedy. When her backpack is so heavy she can't tend to her own burdensome bricks very well at all, it is a good and kind thing to link arms and walk with her through that pain in whatever way feels manageable for you.

However, if the neighbor lady is still calling you twelve months later and asking why you haven't come over to walk the dogs or weed the garden, this is something different. If she pleads with you to keep bringing her meals each week because she has not yet found the energy or the healing from her grief to cook for herself, you've got a problem in the form of an unhealthy exchange of bricks.

It is our responsibility to tend to our *own* bricks. It's that simple. Asking for help from time to time is one thing. But expecting that other people should or will fix the wounds that have been punched through us, especially those from earlier times in our lives, is toxic and damaging, and can quickly snowball into abusive patterns.

When we are willing to get curious about our own bricks and courageous enough to refuse to take on the bricks of others, beautiful interpersonal connection can happen. This process is never without discomfort. But I promise, speaking up for misallocated bricks and breaking this kind of codependent patterning is the stuff miracles are made of.

My marriage to my husband, Matt, is a second marriage for both of us. It didn't take much time at all after we started dating to recognize he had wounds and insecurities around trust and fidelity. To make the situation even trickier, we dated long-distance for the first few years. I lived in Colorado. He lived in Kansas. We worked hard to reserve time to travel and be with each other. And we stayed well connected through calls, emails, texts, and FaceTime dates. But between visits or moments of communication, I continued to engage in my social life, business as usual, including some important friendships with certain men in my life. Everything was on the up and up, and I was forthcoming with all my friends about my newfound love. But the simple fact that I had friends who were men was triggering for Matt.

An extramarital affair broke Matt's first marriage. For a significant amount of time, he was unknowingly on the receiving end of broken vows, twisted truths, left-out information, and outright lies. Because of all this, Matt had some pretty fresh bruises and battle wounds that really started to surface when he and I started dating. At first, I responded by taking on too much responsibility for his pain. I pulled away from some of my male friends. I even boldly told some of them I couldn't be friends with them anymore, not because they (or I) were doing anything wrong, but because it was triggering for my new boyfriend. As a consequence, I hurt and lost connection with good people I cared deeply about. Matt never asked me to do this. My own codependent parts, afraid of losing him or causing him pain, went above and beyond to reduce the risk.

After a while, when Matt's trauma around infidelity was activated, I started to resent the fact I couldn't be myself in my own social network. I felt ashamed I had turned away from and hurt some wonderful people. I eventually decided I wasn't going to do that anymore. There were a few still-standing and particularly important friendships with men I was not willing to part with.

When it was time for this delicate conversation to happen, I turned to the concept and language of the bricks and the backpacks. "I know and respect your pain around infidelity," I told Matt. "I'm so sorry that happened, and I can only imagine the pain you've experienced. And also," I gently added, "it is not okay that I have acquiesced my commitment and dedication to good friendships in an effort to tend to your traumatic brick. I'm not willing to do that anymore." I wanted to honor Matt's pain while also respecting my own boundaries and integrity. "I am not your ex," I told him, "and this is not my brick to carry."

I'm sure I held my breath in anticipation after I said the words out loud. If Matt hadn't known how to fight for his own access to Self-energy, which required a tremendous amount of confidence, calm, and courage, he might have blown through the roof. If he had lost his shit at me, it would not have been because I'd done something wrong. Rather, his reactivity would have been a result of his activated protective parts that so acutely remembered the horrific pain and trauma he had experienced in his previous marriage. Lucky for us both, he was working hard in weekly therapy and had already started to find some healing, along with clarity that his pain was not my responsibility to fix.

Matt and I learned a ton from this conversation. We learned the importance of speaking up when we are feeling burdened by the other person's bricks. We felt the warm embrace of empathy as we listened to each other and owned our own struggles without attacking each other. Above all else, we grew *closer* and *more bonded* with this new realization that we could have real conversations about hard things without taking any of it personally. That kind of intimate closeness and purposeful, meaningful connection served as a safe conduit for loving energy, holding a healthy space while his whole system worked to heal from the brutal trauma of the affair.

Nowadays, Matt and I use the bricks-and-backpacks metaphor on a regular basis. We each work hard to speak up when we recognize we are unfairly expecting the other to tend to our bricks for us. And we have, over time, developed the ability to call each other out when we feel those unhealthy or unfair expectations happening. We use the bricks-and-backpacks language and concept with our kids, in our jobs, and in our friendships.

Getting down the "bricks-and-backpacks" metaphor is an introspective mechanism for clarity, but it's also a vehicle for healthy interpersonal communication. Start by flipping a U-turn and looking inward, calling on your most sincere curiosity, and beginning to familiarize yourself with your own collection of bricks. If you haven't already, start the important work of tending to and healing your bricks so you don't misdirect those burdens onto other people. Up your game around recognizing when you're on the receiving end of expectations to mend someone else's misallocated bricks. Your ability to stand boldly in authenticity and be and feel more yourself is dependent on this kind of clarity and bold communication.

Before dropping my baby brother off at daycare and taking me to elementary school, my mom used to let me watch a little bit of television in the mornings. *Annie* was one of my favorite movies as a kid. One weekday, after I had dressed for school and eaten my breakfast, I sat on the floor in front of the TV wearing my red Smurfs backpack and caught the tail end of the movie. I had seen

Empathy

the film before, so I knew about the whole orphan-to-adoption-by-a-wealthy-bald-guy-who-loved-her-and-wanted-to-become-her-dad thing. It was a rags-to-riches story with a happy ending. But something about the movie's last few minutes hit me in a different way on this particular morning. Annie, in her iconic little, red dress, bounced down the giant, white marble staircase. Then Daddy Warbucks swept her into a carnival celebration with circus tricksters, music, and fireworks, assuring us all that he was going to provide her with a life of love and joy like she never knew was possible.

That morning, as I turned the TV off so we could rush out the front door, I felt a pang of embarrassment and legitimate confusion. There were tears on my cheeks. That last happy scene showing Annie, forever saved from a life of poverty and lovelessness, had tugged on my little seven-year-old heart in a way that made me cry. Up to that point, I had always associated tears with sadness or pain. I didn't understand my emotions in that moment.

I was so happy for Annie that I cried joyful tears. I definitely remember this making me uncomfortable. How strange. I logically knew Annie was a fictional character on television. So why was I feeling her emotions?

I carried that confusing episode around in my memory for decades. At seven years old, I didn't have the vocabulary or understanding to describe, even to myself, what had happened. It wasn't until I started to study the work of Brené Brown that I was able to identify that as a first-grade little girl, I was experiencing this thing we call *empathy*.

In a YouTube animated clip dubbed over with Brené's voice, she shows and describes the important difference between sympathy and empathy. Until viewing this short cartoon, I had never considered that the two concepts were separate or different. As it turns out, sympathy and empathy are quite distinct from one another. And they create significantly varied results when used in interpersonal connection.

"Sympathy," Brené describes, "is feeling *for* someone...Empathy is feeling *with* them." To be with someone in a meaningful way when they are having big feels, we must tap into something within ourselves that is familiar with the emotional experience they are having.

At seven years old, I was just beginning to explicitly notice and feel the effects of having a dad who wasn't emotionally or energetically available for me. Something inside me could relate to Annie's situation, not because I was an orphan, but because I was a little girl who desperately craved the affection and adoration of a dad. When Daddy Warbucks set aside his attachments to wealth and power to show up as a loving and doting father to Annie, I felt her happiness. I felt her joy. Most of all, I felt her relief.

I've known the profound joy of finding out I'm pregnant with my first baby. I've known the excitement of being chosen for a prestigious position after grueling interviews and auditions. I've felt the rush of being in love. I'm all smiles and exuberance when empathy requires I call on those wonderful emotions to help me connect with someone else who is moving through something similar. That's the fun stuff! Tapping into empathy when the emotions involved are uncomfortable, however, is a different story.

Empathy is the reason group therapy, Alcoholics Anonymous meetings, and other similar interpersonal support methods are so effective. I remember walking into my first Al-Anon meeting in my late twenties. Al-Anon is designed to support and create community among individuals whose loved ones struggle with alcoholism. The people in this first meeting didn't know me. They didn't know my story. How could they possibly understand how I feel or even begin to relate to me? That feeling of disconnection and discomfort only increased when I walked in, sat down, and took inventory of the room. I looked at the ten people sitting in chairs set up in a circle in the basement of a church down the road from my house. I didn't speak during that first Al-Anon meeting. I just listened. I felt so broken, lost, and alone that I didn't believe anyone could reach me down deep in that much pain. But as I listened to the other participants speak, I felt they somehow understood me even better than my closest friends.

As the others spoke up about their own situations and experiences, I could sense the layers of their pain. I felt a tremendous amount of connection to these people because they understood my feelings in a way nobody without an addicted loved one ever could. With every tear that dropped from their faces as they spoke, I knew they were accessing hurt and helplessness inside themselves. I had felt it too in my own life and experiences with my dad.

When dealing with matters of pain, empathy is far from comfortable. It requires we dig deep into the things we would prefer to avoid. Empathy asks us to flip a U-turn and refeel feelings we've tried so hard to move past or push away.

In the animated YouTube clip about empathy, Brené's voice reminds us how disconnecting it feels when we are in pain, and someone spouts off solutions at us. It feels dismissive when we are having hard emotions and someone tells us to "Look on the bright side" by using statements that start with "At least..." Those are functions of sympathy, not empathy. Brené encourages us to call on courage and step directly into our own darkness so we can be down in the muck with another human. That is where true, deep connection happens. This is the place where a person in struggle stops feeling quite so alone. Empathy is powerful. It is the thing that shows "*I see you.*"

So what happens when someone sitting across from us is struggling and we can't relate because we've never found ourselves in that same kind of situation? This happens to me all the time in therapy sessions with clients. A woman will be courageously spilling her guts about a horrific sexual assault. (Sometimes, in moments like this, I have to remind myself to stay present and mindful to keep my jaw from dropping to the ground and saying stupid things like, "WTF?" People's stories...man, I tell you.) I know how lucky I am that I've never been sexually assaulted. So how in the world am I supposed to relate to that kind of experience?

Just because I've never been the victim of a sexual violation doesn't mean I don't know what it's like to feel helpless and scared. Now, in no way can I claim to know *that* type or level of distress. Moments like that require me, as a therapist, to call upon fear in the most intense form that I do know it. I know the physical feeling of pumping adrenaline. I know what it feels like to be caught off guard and sense I am possibly in danger. Beyond that, my imagination has to take me as far as it is able in an attempt to wonder what it might have felt like for that client. We must be brave enough to try putting ourselves in their shoes.

Where my wherewithal ends, curiosity kicks in. When I don't know, I ask. There is an incredible amount of power in the question, "What was it like to be you in that moment?" When you are gifted with answers to questions as bold as this, do *not* take it lightly, and do *not* come with agenda. Engage from a place of pure curiosity. It is so important to understand that this person's experience is their true reality, regardless of how rational it may or may not be. The magic of connection happens when we acknowledge their pain for exactly the way they describe it. This is true *especially* when it doesn't make sense to us or is beyond our comprehension.

It has been a long-running tradition in my family to smash cake in the face of whoever's birthday it is. We've been shoving our kids' faces into cakes since their first birthdays. (Don't freak out, it's not as aggressive as it sounds.) My mom has become the primary sneak-attack culprit of making sure the birthday kid ends up with cake up their nose before the night is over. When it's one of the grandkids' birthdays, they keep a keen eye on Grandma all night long. For the most part, it's funny. Most of the kids see it as a hilarious game. However, my son Beckham has always been the exception to the shenanigan. Since a very early age, Beckham has struggled with a powerful trigger around embarrassment.

For years, I've helped Beckham dodge this messy birthday surprise because I know (in a way nobody else understands) how truly upsetting this kind of thing is for him. Last night, Grandma came over for dinner and decided to make up for lost time with Beckham. She snuck up behind him with a handful of chocolate cake while we were sitting around the dinner table, and she smeared it all over his face. Cream cheese frosting was in his ears, down his neck, in his eyes, and definitely up his nose. Everyone else busted out laughing, knowing it was a long time coming. But I knew better than to laugh. At eleven years old, Beckham is the youngest in the family. He avoids feeling embarrassed at all costs. It is one of his most vulnerable exiles. To make matters worse, he has recently become more keenly aware of his fourteen-year-old sister's cute, teeny-bopper friends, one of whom happened to be having dinner with us last night. I knew as soon as it happened that we were about to have an emotional train wreck of an issue on our hands.

Beckham immediately ran into the bathroom and locked the door. I gave him a minute, then knocked and asked if I could come in. The kid was pissed. He yelled back at me and told me to go away. Twenty minutes later, he was finally willing to let me into the bathroom. I sat down on the floor and asked if he wanted to talk. I tried to keep it conversational and asked him if he could tell me what he was feeling. "Embarrassed and angry. She shouldn't have done that," he said through gritted teeth.

His intense reaction was nowhere near rational. Trigger reactions rarely are. If someone had shoved cake in my face, I don't know that I would have been especially thrilled about it. But I certainly would not be so upset I would clench my fists, cry, and lock myself in the bathroom. Since my own emotional reaction would not have been like his, I had to call upon my own experiences of feeling extreme embarrassment in order to identify with my son. I absolutely have a memory or two that bring back that feeling of intense irritation and humiliation. Even thinking about those memories reminds me of the desire to crawl under the covers and hide from the world. When Beckham was brave enough to tell me his feelings, I took it upon myself to remember what the experience of humiliation feels like. The only words that came out of my mouth were, "I get it."

This was enough to get his hard feelings to shift just a bit. It didn't make the experience or his big emotions go away, but it helped Beckham feel seen and heard. At that, he crawled into my lap and wrapped his arms around my neck.

I'm pretty decent at practicing empathy with my clients because that's kind of what I get paid to do. And I'm naturally fairly gentle with my kids and nieces. But rubber sure does seem to meet the road when it comes to extending empathy to other people in my life, especially adults. In my stubbornness, sometimes I forget grown-ups need to be on the receiving end of compassion too. The utilization of empathy requires vulnerable participation. That feels particularly cringy in moments involving friction and hostility. If you are anything like me, you aren't especially fond of vulnerability in situations of conflict. In the spirit of shaking things up and evolving yourself and your relationships, this discomfort is exactly where we need to go.

Ugh, not gonna lie, this part sucks.

When there is tense energy between two or more people or groups, our default is to blend right up with our protective parts. We call on our point-proving, deflective, and defensive parts. Or we rely on avoidant, minimizing, self-shaming, and codependent parts. If we are feeling really backed into a corner, we might even blend with attacking parts that want to wound the other side. Extending curiosity or vulnerability is the furthest thing from what feels natural. This makes total sense when you think of it from a trauma and nervous-system perspective. Remember the snake and the garden hose?

When we step into conflict, our amygdala is chomping at the bit to fire into action. It can't wait to pull the plug on our prefrontal ability to think logically. It doesn't want us to regulate our emotions. Remember, it thinks any kind of vulnerability is the enemy. All the amygdala cares about is defending and protecting you. Meaningful interpersonal connection is nowhere on the amygdala's radar. It does not care about conflict resolution, interpersonal connection, or anything that resembles calm. The amygdala's only interests are your safety and survival. A working understanding and disciplined utilization of an empathetic skillset can work wonders in moments of intensity or argument.

A great way to hone your empathy skills is to practice using the words, "Tell me more." This is true whether a connection involves conflict or not. "Tell me more," lets the other person know you are willing to step into curiosity for the sake of understanding their perspective more accurately. "Tell me more," is the opposite of defensiveness, avoidance, or blame and attack. When asked sincerely, it lets the other person know they matter. Even if you have to say it through gritted teeth during an argument, get the words out, and try to mean them. Be open to the response. Stay out of the temptation to take anything personally, stand firm in your integrity, and focus on practicing empathy. This change in the way you fight will alter the outcome for the better. It will also support your ability to feel less charged during conflict.

Empathy is almost completely an inside job, so mindfulness is key. Lucky for us all (especially since empathy isn't always naturally occurring), this set of skills can be learned, taught, and

practiced. We can get better at empathy. If honing your empathetic abilities with real-life interactions freaks you out, start by
practicing with fictional characters.

Little Fires Everywhere, by Celeste Ng, is a 2017 novel that was
later made into a TV miniseries starring Reese Witherspoon.
Elena Richardson, the character played by Witherspoon, has
some obviously overfunctioning parts. Elena is the mom with
the large, pristine house, a perfectly dry-cleaned and ironed
wardrobe, and Christmas cards that go out on time every year
like clockwork. She keeps color coded calendars hung on the
kitchen wall to inform each family member of exactly when
and where they need to be throughout the week. She's catty and
gossipy. She has strong judgments against one of her daugh-
ters, who rebels against the picture-perfect, cookie-cutter life
being provided to her. Elena's judgmental and controlling parts
dictate her energy and behaviors most of the time, especially
when she's under stress. In many ways, she's a tough character
to like. However, the author and film creators did a beautiful job
of inviting the readers and viewers into a state of empathy for
this character by floating back in time to show Elena's earlier life
experiences. This gives us a unique glimpse into why she functions the way she does.

When reading and seeing the pain this character experienced
in her past, her current-day judgmental and controlling parts
start to make a lot of sense. The perspective doesn't justify
her dysfunctional behaviors. But it does make her choices and
emotional reactions click together like puzzle pieces and helps
us understand the bigger picture. The readers and viewers of
Little Fires Everywhere don't get that gift of understanding without the energy of empathy. By showing Elena's past struggles,

it pulls us into feeling *with* her. Seeing her in pain during her younger years is relatable. It reminds us all about the hard things we've felt during certain times in our own lives. It bonks us on the head with a remembrance of our own humanity. This character's behaviors are often far from stellar. At times, they are outright offensive and abusive. But knowing her backstory helps us stay in a state of open-mindedness and become able to consider that perhaps this woman is doing the best she can with what she knows.

Extending empathy does not mean we let people off the hook for dysfunction. Boundaries and accountability are still incredibly important. But those things are about something else. Boundaries combined with empathy differentiates between a solid, steel door of disconnection and the transparent screen door that allows for a loving and mutual respect for humanness to flow through. Empathy is about connection. It is about remembering we are all human and we all struggle.

So the next time your teenage daughter is an irrational, emotional wreck over the fact that she can't find her favorite jeans, or your friend on social media is frantically posting political articles that feel full of conspiracy theories, remember, there are reasons why they think and feel the way they do. They are having big emotions inside themselves that they are struggling to regulate. It may make zero rational sense. But in the spirit of connection, that's not the most important part. What helps connection is your recognition that the pain is *real* for them.

Challenge yourself to consider what others are feeling inside. Open your mind to the possibility that they might be doing the best they can. Welcome their big feels with curiosity and the invitation, "Tell me more." When we talk about putting ourselves in someone else's shoes, don't just *think* about what it might be like to be them. Instead, allow yourself to *feel* what it might be like. Call upon those feelings inside yourself and keep your own words to a minimum. If you really need to get in the last word, consider extending gratitude instead of trying to prove the final point. When someone is coming to you from a place of pain, confusion, anger, or fear, don't walk away without saying, "Thank you for sharing your perspective with me."

Great connection with other people isn't great because it's always clean and easy. The best, most impactful relationships and interactions are often those that involve vulnerability, perspective taking, and (in the case of conflict) a willingness to consider *you* might be wrong.

When I was a kid, I had a black cat named Pepper. She'd run around in the

Willing to Be Wrong

woods behind our house chasing mice and fighting possums. That cat was sweet as sugar with us (her humans) but tough as nails when she needed to protect herself. When Pepper got angry or scared, the fur down the back of her neck would stand on end. Even after the threat was gone, she'd stay jumpy for a bit. Small, unexpected noises or movements would make the mohawk stand right back up. Sometimes, it would take an hour for Pepper to fully calm back down enough for that spike of fur to relax.

I spent the greater part of a decade completely overhauling my life between the ages of thirty and forty. During those years, my protective parts learned to get louder, take up more space, and stop putting up with bullshit. My hypervigilant mohawk, like Pepper's, was up for a long time. It took a while for it to relax. Toward the end of my thirties and into my forties, I'm slowly learning that my revised life and relationships are now a safe place to be. It has become okay for my sharpened claws to relax and retract a bit. But if my system picks up on potential risks of feeling unheard, disrespected, under-valued, or taken advantage of (exiles that kept me in a state of chronic codependency for way too long), the hair on the back of my neck stands on end. This protective response makes it really hard for me to consider I might be in the wrong, especially during a moment of conflict.

Perspective taking requires we suspend our own certainty and attachment to our opinions and perceptions long enough to allow true consideration of someone else's. Our mind correlates surrender with defeat. And our nervous system connects vulnerability to risk. Opening our minds up to the possibility that we might be wrong sends signals of danger to the rest of our system. Hanging our hat on our own righteousness isn't just more comfortable, it's hardwired into us as a safety tactic. Yet we know this kind of openness and willingness to be wrong is a linchpin to meaningful human connection. It's quite the conundrum.

The ability to be mindfully aware of this protective phenomenon separates humans from all other living creatures on the planet. The ability to wrestle with reactivity and to instead choose a calm response is a telltale sign of high emotional intelligence. Show me a person who can thoughtfully respond rather than mindlessly react, and I'll show you a person who has done the work!

I've come to think of the practice of perspective taking kind of like trying on clothes, which is not one of my favorite things. My wardrobe is simple and predictable. Sweatpants; dark jeans; white, V-neck T-shirts; and hoodies make up about 80 percent of my closet. Clothes shopping feels a little bit like torture to me. I know what I like, and I'm comfortable with what's familiar to me. Plus, my limited energy and time are already accounted for in other areas of my life. So walking into a store, trying on clothes, and spending hours conceptualizing new outfits is just not my jam.

Much to my chagrin, when I do finally replace wardrobe pieces that have worn out or don't fit me well anymore, I always find I feel better. Last fall, I threw away a pair of jeans that had been my favorite for years. The new pair I replaced them with was a little stiffer than I prefer and hasn't yet washed out to the color I like. But on the upside, now nobody can see my underwear through paper-thin denim when I bend over. That step out of what's familiar and into a phase of adjustment isn't usually (ever?) comfortable. But it is sometimes necessary because the old and outdated can't sustain your forward movement.

I bet we can all think of an example that required us to challenge our own righteousness in order to grow. Here's one of mine. I grew up in the Lutheran church. I adored the old, traditional hymns, the stained glass windows, and the bell choir. Then I spent my twenties and early thirties submerged in the world of non-denominational Christianity. The church was a family to me. For the first thirty-five years of my life in these environments, I was taught and told that LGBTQ+ "choices" and "lifestyles" were a sin. The message was clear. Anything other than binary gender identification and monogamous heterosexuality was wrong and bad. I grew up going to school in the conservative community of Tecumseh, Kansas. At that time, there was a clear line drawn in the sand between us heterosexuals and the "other" people who believed it was okay to live in so-called defiance and wretchedness.

Later, as an adult, various people in my life challenged my us-versus-them mentality and my Christian-based perception that homosexuality was wrong. For the longest time, I refused to listen. I had closed my mind off to the idea *I* might be wrong or my own perspectives needed an update. I had known people who embraced the LGBTQ+ community, then experienced a loss of their church community. I felt afraid of that. My resistance to considering another perspective came from a desire to avoid possible ostracization from my beloved community and stick with what was familiar and comfortable.

Until it wasn't comfortable anymore.

Something deep inside my guts started to churn around this topic. As an identifying Christian at the time, I was taught to be inclusive and loving to *all*. I was supposed to be *nonjudgmental*. Yet here were these rules around gender identity and sexuality that were resulting in an othering factor inside myself supported by the church's perspectives. It didn't feel good.

I spent a few years opening my ears and mind to the other perspectives. I spoke with friends, family, and clients who identify outside the straight and narrow cisgender and hetero-sexual lanes. I heard a repertoire of stories and emotional experiences that differed from my own and definitely strayed from what I had been taught through the church and the mentalities of my conservative community.

Then one day, I got called to the table because of a response I had posted to something on Facebook. With my words, I had claimed any variation in sexuality or gender identification was a wrong and bad thing. This alienated the loving energy and unconditional positive regard for others I ordinarily tried to project. Someone called me a hypocrite.

My natural defense, because I don't like being called names and I really don't like being told I'm wrong, was to lash out. The hair on the back of my neck stood up, and my point-proving parts took over. I responded by quoting Christian scripture at them and relied on black-and-white thinking to justify my perspective. I spouted the narrative that had been hammered into me throughout my entire life. I was right; they were wrong, and they needed to know about it.

But then, I still felt shitty. It felt like my jeans had been shrunk in the wash and were now two sizes too small, but I was refusing to acknowledge the dissonance and squeezing into them anyway. The feeling was tolerable enough and probably could have been swept under the rug or distracted away by putting the blinders back on and going about my life. But something in me knew this issue would boil just under the surface until I faced it head on.

Around this time, I was in a season of taking inventory and doing away with all things that no longer fit or served my ability to thrive. This ten-year deconstruction period of life included the shedding of relationships, certain foods, old shoes, bad habits, and (the toughest of the spring cleaning) certain belief patterns. It was clear my old beliefs about sexuality and gender identity were causing me discomfort, and they were hurting other people. So I decided to do the U-turn, get real curious, and show up for the rumble.

I reflected on the experiences from those people I had already spoken to. I started exposing myself to more stories, art, and works from people within the LGBTQ+ community. And I got proactive about asking questions to more folks who identified in different ways than I did. The more questions I asked, the more sincerely curious I felt. When checking my integrity, I knew, without a shadow of a doubt, that othering was not okay with me. Nonjudgment and radical acceptance had become two hell-yes components that lived within my circle of integrity. They served as a foundation for the way I wanted to live life and the person I wanted to be in the world. My old beliefs about sexuality and gender identity did not sync up with my evolving integrity. The person challenging me on Facebook had been correct. I *was* being hypocritical!

This was an "Oh shit" moment for me. I knew my shift would fly in the face of many Christian friends and family members I loved and respected. At the time, I had become an integrated part of a church family here in Denver. This organization helped support my psychotherapy private practice by referring clients to me. By stepping into my integrity and out of my old biases around sexuality and gender identification, I was afraid those referrals would stop, and *I* would be othered by the church I loved so much. Unfortunately, in the end, those fears did come true.

A representative from the church called to tell me I was being removed from their mental healthcare provider list because I refused to stand against LGBTQ+ "behaviors and lifestyles." I couldn't believe how quickly I was pushed to the outside by my own church community. It was hurtful. But, even amid that pain and rejection, I knew choosing to embrace the fact that I had been wrong for all those years was the only way to recover my own ultimate okayness.

I had been holding on to an old bias that was no longer supporting my integrity. I said some "I'm sorry"s, and I started aligning my thoughts and actions with my growing convictions around inclusivity, radical acceptance, and love toward all. Acknowledging my ignorance, biases, and the need for a reroute gave me freedom I hadn't realized I'd been denying myself. With my integrity now intact, the reward was greater than the pain of the loss of that church family. Now, when this topic arises, I am solid in clarity and confidence that I am functioning in alignment with my integrity. I can't say it was without pain and an epic dose of humility. But I can wholeheartedly report it was worth it.

Sometimes the department-store sales associate will bring you an outfit you never would have picked off the rack for yourself. These come in the form of people's perceptions, opinions, choices, and lifestyles that feel unfamiliar, irrational, and, sometimes, outright offensive. It is important to recognize that just because a perspective doesn't align with your way of doing things doesn't make it wrong. It certainly doesn't mean varying perspectives don't deserve to be considered.

When a new opportunity or perspective is introduced to us, we unconsciously do an instantaneous scan through our mind, body, and heart to see what activates. In a millisecond, parts that want to protect and inform us say, "Hey, this reminds me of so-and-so," or, "Way-back-when," or, "Such and such." These parts want us to recollect something we've heard, learned, or lived through and use it as a reference. This is the moment when, if you are awake and aware, you have an opportunity to grow. You can get curious about your triggers, encourage your protective parts to step aside when the waters of conflict are rising, and make the courageous choice to expand your perceptions. These are the moments when you can look at the foreign and bizarre shirt brought to you by the department-store salesperson and say, "Sure, why not? Let's give it a try."

Most often, taking something off the hanger to try on isn't dangerous. Remember, you don't have to buy the shirt, take it home, and wear it every day. It is okay to try it on and decide you'd prefer not to purchase it at all. On its own, the process of purposefully venturing out of your comfort zone will expand you in ways that aren't otherwise possible, regardless of what ultimately ends up feeling true for you. And in the spirit of interpersonal connection, your willingness to try on other perspectives will increase the level of meaningful synergy between you and other people. At worst, you decide the new perspective isn't for you, but at least you can say you gave it a go. Your level of appreciation for diversity will expand, and the hairs on the back of your neck will, on average, tend to stay more relaxed.

At best, every so often, you'll realize a shirt you'd never have otherwise considered has become one of your favorite go-to pieces. No matter where you ultimately land, you will grow from a disposition of willingness to consider your own perceptions, opinions, judgments, or beliefs might be wrong, outdated, damaging, or hurtful to others. That kind of openness will draw people to you. You'll have more credibility and be on the receiving end of increased respect and kindness. When you truly and vulnerably consider differing perspectives, it says to someone else, "You matter; I see you, and I care." At the end of the day, I wonder if *that* is perhaps more important than staying comfortable or being right.

Particularly when dealing in relationships with others, there's a really simple way to determine whether you are functioning from a place of closed-mindedness or curiosity.

Count the question marks.

If true connection is your honest motive, then your inner and outer dialogues will be full of question

Use More Question Marks

marks. Remember, there is a difference between pure curiosity and asking questions doused in agenda. We can *feel* agenda, even if it is sneakily hidden in the energy behind the words. We can also *feel* openness and sincerity. The contrast is palpable. So these can't be just any ol' question marks. They must be earnest ones backed by nothing other than an authentic desire to better understand someone.

Written communication is probably the most obvious place to start this exploration. Pull up an old text, letter, or email you either wrote or received in a moment of stressful interaction. Observe the punctuation. Are there significantly more periods or question marks?

It feels good to be around people who are intentional about asking sincere questions. It's nice when someone seems interested in hearing about our thoughts, opinions, feelings, and experiences. It makes us feel worthy of being seen and known. The best mentors, bosses, coaches, and parents use more question marks than periods. Think back through your life. Who are the people you've felt best around? Are those folks the ones who crammed their own opinions down your throat? Or were they people who tended to be generous with their usage of question marks?

There is certainly a time and place for giving advice or instruction. Just be consciously mindful of those times by noticing whether or not you've been *asked* for guidance or your opinion. My daughter works with a math tutor, for example. By hiring the woman who helps her, we have implicitly said, "We trust your expertise and ability to provide instruction. Will you please help us?" Similarly, when a friend comes to you and asks what you would you do in their position, they are expecting some statements with periods at the end of them. They are asking for help, opinions, and guidance.

Consider when people come to us sharing their own thoughts, feelings, or experiences, and we talk back *at* them without offering curiosity. We give solutions and advice, even though we haven't been asked for it. We provide the opinions and responses *we* would choose if we were in their shoes without an invitation to do so. Or we offer up stories of a time when we were in a similar situation, assuming our own experience and resolution are what they need to hear. We project. We believe, perhaps, this is the best way to relate to this person. Isn't that interesting? I wonder, do we do that so the other person can feel better? Or do we project because it feels good to us?

During interpersonal communication and connection, it is wise to refrain from jumping to conclusions about what the other person is needing or expecting and instead just *ask*. For instance, if one of my employees steps into my office and banters about a certain experience they are having with a client, it is tempting to assume they want my advice. I sometimes make that same assumption if my teenage daughter comes home from school and talks for twenty minutes about a complex social interaction she's having with friends, or my husband tells me about a tricky business dynamic he's experiencing with a colleague. Rather than jumping into advice-giving mode, I've found it super helpful to respond with a reflective observation followed by a question. "Sheesh, that sounds really tough. Is there anything you need from me that might feel helpful?"

Using a question mark in this way accomplishes two really important things. It tells the person, "I see you, and I honor the way you are feeling right now." That alone is *huge* in terms of meaningful interpersonal connection! The second thing of value is it puts the power back in their hands to inform you of their needs. This keeps you from stepping into assumptions. They can respond by saying, "I could really use some advice," "I'd just appreciate a hug," or "I don't think I need anything from you. I'm just grateful you are willing to listen."

If, in a moment like this, they respond with, "I don't know what I need," that's an awesome opportunity for you to use more question marks. Encourage their own mindfulness. Empower them to explore their own inner experience. Instead of telling them what you believe they should feel, think, or do, extending curiosity will hold them accountable for shifting out of "I don't know," and into self-exploration and advocacy. By throwing statements at them, we take away the opportunity for them to do something brilliant or comforting for themselves. Question marks tell them, "I believe in you and your ability to move through this."

The stereotype of therapists is that we are constantly asking, "How does that make you feel?" There's good reason for that. We are trying to prompt a U-turn and guide you toward a mindful observation of your inner experience. Therapists are not supposed to be advice givers. If we tell you what we think you should do, we are inserting our own biased agenda into your life experience. That's not cool. Plus, it creates a mess around ownership of consequences and outcomes, for better or worse. If a client takes a therapist's advice, acts on it, and has a poor outcome, the therapist is partially to blame for that. Similarly, if a therapist offers up a solution that ends up turning out well for the client, at least part of the ownership of that success goes to the therapist. That takes away the client's knowledge that they are capable of making good choices for themselves. It takes away a slice of their autonomy and personal agency.

Curiosity really is the most incredible conduit for interpersonal connection. Can you imagine how the social climate of our country and world would shift if everyone began using more question marks than periods? Surround yourself with people who are generous with their curious punctuation, know how and when to shut their mouths and listen, and place their focus on empowering you to create your own solutions. Simultaneously, go out into the world and direct that same kind of energy toward others. It will feel different. Maybe uncomfortable at first. But I believe, with my whole heart, you'll grow quite fond of the bonding results you will ultimately get to experience.

There are parts of me that hate it when people don't like me. There, I said it.

I'm sure there are psychological reasons related to my attachment trauma that can explain exactly why this is such a hot button for me. You can add to the equation that I was a dancer for the first thirty years of my life before transitioning into a career that involves speaking on stages in

I'm Not for Everyone

front of audiences. Performing is in my blood. It's a lifelong, reinforced piece of how I'm built. Ideally, the point of performing for an audience is to create a meaningful experience for others. That doesn't work very well if you've got a crowd full of critics and haters.

To anyone reading this who claims, "I don't care what other people think," I call baloney. You may have some strong protective parts that excel at compartmentalizing or pushing other people's opinions about you aside. But unless you are a bona fide sociopath, you absolutely have parts of yourself that *do* care what other people think. Have you ever smiled and nodded even though you had no idea what was being said? Do you double-check to make sure your fly's zipped before you leave the bathroom? Do you ever check your social media posts to see if anyone has liked or commented on them? See? You care.

Some sense of awareness about how others perceive you is healthy and totally normal. But when we care too much, we risk alienating our authentic selves. Everyone who has dared to pursue self-actualization will tell you there's no such thing as a foolproof fan base. The more boldly true you are to yourself, the more critics you are guaranteed to have. This is especially true if your pursuit for realness goes against a cultural norm or the strong convictions of others.

About midway through my ten-year personal reconciliation process, I stumbled across a quote by poet Alexandra Elle. I wrote it on a sticky note and for many years kept it where I could read it every day. It has become my motto, steadily running through my mind like a ticker tape:

> I am not afraid of my truth anymore, and I will not omit pieces of myself to make you more comfortable.

Elle's words give me permission to be unapologetically myself. It is a reminder that authenticity is my North Star. That quote empowers and inspires me while offering a gentle but clear challenge to my codependency-based parts.

Nowadays, I no longer give nearly as much energy to playing games of conformity. It doesn't cause me pause or sway if I find joy in something that other people don't. I still love and listen to the music of Green Day. I eat ketchup on green beans. I buzzed all my hair off on my fortieth birthday. I openly display my tattoos and piercings. I wear shorts on hot days, even though my legs are nowhere near in the same kind of shape as when I was younger. I suppose I've learned to handle a few raised eyebrows. I now recognize people's judgment of me as a reflection of their own insecurities and lack of open-mindedness.

I am conscious of how I show up in the world for different reasons now. It is less about meeting other people's expectations, and more about aligning with my own integrity, values, and personal purpose. Because I understand nothing is personal, I don't usually give people's judgments of me more than a quick moment of my time or headspace. Instead, I reroute and devote that energy toward beautiful things—solutions, creativity, innovation, greater clarity in knowing myself, and practice in the areas of patience, forgiveness, and grace.

I'm dedicated to saying what I mean and meaning what I say. I speak up when something feels crummy to me. I have a low tolerance for sugary sweetness, inauthentic excessive enthusiasm, or phony kindness, especially when my people-pleasing parts threaten to steer my own personality in that direction.

If we truly believe that the most authentic version of ourselves is also the most optimized one, we can't hold too tightly onto the desire for people to like us. Trust that the most real and true *you* is the one that will serve the world the best. Your authenticity is more important than your ability to avoid pissing people off.

When something isn't okay with you, don't pretend it is. Don't say yes when you mean no. I spent the first thirty years of my life hijacked by desperately overfunctioning codependent parts. Now, at this point in my life, I have lost all interest in trying to adapt to other people's expectations. The relationships I value are those in which I can safely speak up when something has been said or done that feels crappy. I only engage in close friendships with people who are willing to listen without getting reactive. I refuse to spend my limited time or bandwidth on relationships with people who make or take things personally. There is very little freedom to be yourself within dynamics like that.

The commitment to authenticity requires that we eradicate fakeness. I have known so many people who keep their mouths shut when something doesn't feel okay to them. They are afraid of rocking the boat or potentially causing someone else discomfort. You don't have to avoid hard conversations with people who are emotionally healthy, know how to self-regulate, and are able to stay out of reactivity. With those folks, you can be real. You can be yourself. Surround yourself, collaborate, and do life with *those* people.

Being unapologetically raw and real comes with consequences. Reactivity is, unfortunately, the norm in our culture. When most of us were kids, we didn't have healthy influences teaching us about emotional self-regulation. So now, here we are, grown-ass adults trying to figure out the tug-of-war between wanting to be authentic and wanting people to like us.

Here's an example. About two months into the COVID-19 experience in the late spring of 2020, I received a text from a friend asking if something was wrong. This is a gal who I had met a couple years prior. Her family and mine had grown close and spent a significant amount of time doing life together over the previous two years. When the shit storm of 2020 began, it became apparent (in ways that it hadn't been possible to see before) that we didn't see eye to eye on some things.

Generally speaking and outwardly facing, this woman is kind. She is a compassionate and smart human. The fact that we had differing opinions in a few areas of life really didn't bother me much until a disrespectful post showed up on her Instagram account. It was insensitive and said unkind things about people who share my own perspective on the approach to combating the COVID-19 virus.

Looking back now with hindsight, I recognize there were about a half dozen other little pink flags I'd turned a blind eye to until that day when she asked me if there was an issue. If I had said, "Nope, everything is cool," it would have been a bald-faced lie. I didn't have total clarity at that point on why I had been feeling discomfort in our friendship except for that hurtful social media post. So my answer to her questions was:

> Yes, something feels yucky. Your Instagram post felt hurtful, disrespectful, and dismissive. I've picked up on tension between us too, but I can't quite put my finger on exactly what it's all about. The differences in our belief systems are likely just surfacing because of the intense feelings that the events of 2020 are bringing up for almost everyone. I don't agree with everything you say and do. However, I respect

your opinions, and I value you as a person. I think the angst we are both noticing is likely just a natural byproduct of this crazy moment in time and the differences that are coming into the light because of it. I'm not worried about our friendship. I love you and care about you. But I do think it would be smart for us to create just a little space while we all adjust and learn to navigate this very weird experience.

Oh shit, man. After I sent that response, you'd have thought I'd kidnapped their family dog and sold him to the highest bidder to make a few bucks so I could buy myself a new pair of Jordans. My response to her question did not sit well with her. All of a sudden, she claimed I had made it difficult for her to sleep at night and had allegedly broken her heart.

I was legitimately confused at this response. Here I was thinking I was communicating clearly, authentically, and with kindness. I put love and courage at the forefront, and I did my best to answer her questions with clarity and truth. Her reaction definitely did not seem to match the situation. I recognize when a person asks if something is wrong, they aren't hoping for an affirmative answer. But doesn't it seem logical that if they are going to ask the question, they are truly curious about whether or not there's a rift?

I maneuvered my thoughts through an integrity checklist. Had I been honest? Yes. Had I stayed calm? Yes. Did I communicate clearly that I cared for her and respected her differing opinions? Yes. Was I empathetic about her desire for me to understand her opinions? Yes (to the point that I'd spent hours watching every documentary and reading every article she had sent me in an attempt to consider her perspectives). Did I ask questions to clarify anything that felt confusing to me? Yes. Was I staying out of the temptation to take it personally or absorb it as an attack on my own character? Yes.

I gave her an honest answer while leaving my sword and shield on the ground. I offered up space as well as ways to possibly move forward. Ultimately, however, she decided to disconnect completely from me, my family, and every friend she knew through me. There was no attempt to talk through a solution or communicate new, helpful boundaries. No value placed on the previous years of friendship. In the couple years since then, my handful of attempts at friendly outreach (to say, "Hello," "Thinking about you," or "Happy birthday,") have been ignored. No acknowledgment or reply. Just avoidant silence. Ghosted.

In the end, I don't know exactly why she chose to end the friendship. Perhaps she doesn't want to spend time with people who don't think like she does. Perhaps she doesn't want to participate in relationships with people who speak up when she's said or done something hurtful. Or maybe it's none of that. Maybe she just plain doesn't like me. It might be that simple.

This was not the first time something like this happened. I would love to say every time I speak my truth, the outcome always results in better understanding and a more bonded sense of connection. But some people don't know what to do with that kind of transparency. The more you come to know yourself and step out of the shadows, the more clear you will become about what's not okay with you. The more you commit to authentic living, the more you will put yourself at risk of rejection, judgment, and loss. I wish it weren't that way. But in our broken humanness, the risk is inevitable.

Throughout my journey of getting clear about who I am and what is important to me, I've had people react with judgment to how I dress, parent my kids, cut my hair, run my business, and much, much more. Your authenticity *is* going to sit well with *some* people. In fact, it will inspire some folks and give them permission to be real and honest in their own lives. For others, it will trigger the ever-loving shit out of their own fears and insecurities. It's real messy, this whole authenticity thing.

If you want to live in alignment with your truest sense of Self, I implore you to get a little more comfortable with the fact that you will not be everyone's cup of tea. If you think differently than someone else, you are a perceived threat to their own certainty. If something about the way you show up in the world differs from what they believe to be right, true, or good, that dissonance makes them compare the way you do things to the way they do things. In our culture, we assume, all too often, that *different* equals *wrong*. I just don't think most people are equipped to wrestle with uncertainty or their own insecurities in the way being confronted with varying perspectives requires.

Now we've acknowledged the most authentic version of you won't have a universal fan club. What about the parts of life that require you to interact with individuals who *you* don't jive with?

Many parents teach their kids to be friends with everyone. The intention behind that guidance is loving and inclusive. But it sends the message that our children need to pretend they like everyone, even if they don't. That's not authentic. It is possible to value another human and show them respect and kindness without having to like them or feel a desire to spend time with them. Some people just don't vibe with each other for a multitude of reasons. There's nothing wrong with that. Keep your thoughts and behaviors within your integrity. And look for the good in others while simultaneously maintaining your boundaries. Then you can have *love* for every person from a humanistic perspective while accepting the reality that you may not *like* them. You can still be cordial, smile, and say hello but refrain from making plans to hang out with them. It is possible to dislike someone without acting like an asshole toward them. Giving ourselves these permissions takes the pressure off and allows us to focus on being authentic and true to our own core identities, which ultimately is the most loving thing for everyone involved.

I would love to feel certain that every one of my ex-boyfriends, ex-colleagues, or ex-bosses thinks highly of me. In a dream world, every past friend, roommate, neighbor, classmate, and colleague would regard me with unconditional respect and believe I'm awesome. Unfortunately, I know better than to hold my breath for that fantasy to become reality.

Right around the time when that friendship was unraveling, I stumbled across a digital ad for a super-cute, terry-cloth, gray sweatshirt. It had red heart patches on the elbows and screen-printed black letters across the front that read, "I'm not for everyone." When I tried that phrase on for size, something about it gave me peace. It felt like an acceptance of a thing I couldn't change anyway, no matter how much I wanted to. It was a release of the expectation that everyone *should* like me. It gave me permission to take a breath and stop worrying what that friend or anyone else potentially assumes to be true about me.

When I put my head on my pillow to sleep at night, I can usually say my intentions have been good and I've made choices that align with my integrity. I am imperfect, and I screw up all the time. But I'll own that and apologize when necessary. The commitment to stay awake, aware, and mindful of others while maintaining tenacity in this lifelong pursuit of personal growth is more important to me than any other person's opinion of me. *That* is the best I can do. If it's not enough for someone else, eh, okay.

After years and years of utilizing U-turns and curiosity through therapy and self-work, I have finally come home to the acceptance that *I'm not for everyone.* You won't be either. If you know yourself well, function within your integrity, are rooted in a foundation of love, and still have a few critics, take it as a sign you're probably doing something right.

Connection to the Bigger Picture

You've now learned a thing or two about zooming in by using introspection and curiosity to connect better with yourself. You've also onboarded some new insight about connecting with other people. Now, in our last section, we're going to zoom way out and consider: why? Who cares? What's the point? Why does any of this matter anyway?

If you've ever laughed until you peed your pants, had a really good cry, felt truly fascinated by something, fallen in love, or grieved so hard you doubted you'd ever recover, then you know. You understand these moments and that what we do with them matters. To *feel* our way through this life is to be fully human and fully alive. Plus, you leave a footprint. Your choices and behaviors influence every person, place, and thing you come in contact with. The way you move through the world creates a ripple effect that, whether you like it or not, does make an impact.

In this third section, we find the connective tissue between our individual existence and the universe we inhabit. Everything we do produces a force elsewhere. It is perhaps the most difficult concept to wrap our heads around because of its enormity and abstraction. This kind of connection is highly spiritual. It involves an intentional consideration about life purpose, alignment, nonattachment, hope, creating meaning, and living in the constant pursuit of joy and connection. Existential exploration requires and evokes the ultimate question marks. The goal is not to find every explicit answer. Rather, we move through this section with the objective of exercising our natural curiosity simply for the sake of being curious. Because that, all on its own, moves us beyond our individual lives and connects us to the bigger picture. What better place to tap into the spirit of curiosity than, once again, through nature.

Uncompahgre Peak is in the San Juan mountain range. Of all the 14ers I've climbed so far, Uncompahgre is my favorite. The afternoon before our hike, Matt and I backpacked in and set our tent up on the outskirts of the forest. Unlike most 14ers, the summit of Uncompahgre is viewable from almost anywhere on the trail once you pass the tree line. We went to sleep at 8 p.m. with the silhouetted peak of our hiking destination looming above us as the sun started to set.

The alarm went off at 2 a.m. Our goal was to hit the summit in time to watch the sun rise over the mountaintops, so the clock was ticking. We slept in most of our hiking clothes and preprepped our backpacks with water, sunscreen, and plenty of snacks. Matt and I threw on our hiking boots and extra layers of clothes before stepping out of the tent under a canopy of black sky and a billion stars. When you get that far off the grid and away from the city lights, the labyrinth of stars is jaw dropping. We stopped hiking multiple times to turn off our headlamps, stand in the blackness of the night, and gaze up into the heavens. That feeling is hard to describe. Awe, I guess, is the most accurate word I can think of to describe it. For a moment, it makes you leave the body you're in and forget everything about your life. It reminds us we are not separate from the infinite vastness of the universe. The experience is such a stark contrast to the myopic, half-blind focus of my own individual existence. It feels good to get lost in encounters like that, allowing nature to absorb me completely.

As we hiked, the light from our head lamps was our only guide, showing us where to step. The lamps were strong enough to shine light on the five feet of ground in front of us, but not more than that. The blackness of the night hid all insight about what lay beyond the ground that we could see under our feet. At times, we could sense our trail ran less than ten feet from the edge where level ground stopped. The open space to our right or left could have been a mild, rolling hill leading down into a field. It was also possible we were walking within feet of sharp, rocky, thousand-foot drop-offs. We knew not to veer from the trail.

Whenever I night hike, I can't help but wonder what's lurking outside the limited circle of light from my headlamp. I fantasize about how big the trees must be, the family of mountain goats sleeping nearby who raise their heads to watch us hike past them, and the millions of wild flowers waiting for the sun to come out so they can wake up and show their colors. The feeling of not knowing what terrain or wildlife may be standing five feet away while hiking through the wilderness is both exhilarating and haunting.

As we hiked Uncompahgre that morning, I remember having an inner conversation with myself about perspective. I recall thinking that sometimes in life, we can't see beyond what's right in front of us. And there's no way to get more insight aside from waiting for time to pass, for something to happen, for the sun to come up. In the darkness, we can keep moving if we want to. It only takes a little light to serve as enough of a guide for us to keep putting one foot in front of the other. The feeling of navigating through one day at a time, especially in the midst of darkness or uncertainty, is daunting. Hell, I've lived through phases of life when I had to focus on getting through one *hour* at a time and pray like crazy I could make it to the end of the day. It is tempting to feel defeated by knowing the world is still turning all around you, for better or worse. It can be intimidating knowing that you have such a tiny radius of purview and control in this big world.

As we neared the top of our hike, the mountain peaks on the horizon started to become visible as silhouettes against the slowly brightening sky. The Earth rotated enough to welcome the first light from the sun. The peaks on the horizon stood black against an only-slightly-less-black sky. One footstep at a time, in some areas having to scramble and climb on all fours, we made it to the summit. Grays and blues followed by pinks and oranges started to reflect off the clouds. While everyone we knew slept in their warm beds at home, Matt and I sat down and ate breakfast at 14,308 feet above sea level. We watched the sun rise over the Rocky Mountains on top of the sixth tallest mountain in the state of Colorado.

Now that the sunshine lit up the Earth all around us, we could see the massive valleys on all sides of our peak. The terrain we had hiked through was no longer a mystery. We could see most of the trail and tell how far we had come over the past few hours. The big hedge of bushes at tree line, where we had stashed our tent and sleeping bags, looked impossibly far away. In the new light, we could see herds of fluffy mountain goats chomping away at the grass in the open valleys. We had likely walked right past them in the dark.

It was only in this moment, after the climb, that we were able to see all that we had navigated through. The hindsight was fascinating. When we had sensed a change in the terrain, we had been correct. At times, we had been walking just feet from giant cliff edges. During other sections along the trail, the openness had been a rolling transition from the rocky dirt path under our feet into humongous fields of sprawling wildflowers. From our sunrise vantage point perched on the summit, we now had the full understanding of how much we had moved through in the dark. Indeed, the sunlight enabled us to zoom out and see the whole picture.

The descending hike was just as fun as the climb up, but in a completely different way. Now, with this zoomed-out perspective, our focus changed. The breathtaking, star-speckled canopy had morphed into a blue sky full of fluffy, white clouds and sunshine. We could see miles and miles into the distance. Our earlier, limited knowledge of what stood a few feet from us now extended boundlessly in all directions. We could see the stretch of the San Juans' beauty.

Bucketloads of valuable experiences came from both perspectives: walking in the dark and retracing our steps in the light. If we'd waited until the sun was up to start the hike, we'd have missed the experience of hiking under the stars and the exciting mystery about what lay in the shadows around us. If we had stayed in the dark, zoomed-in to the five-foot radius of visibility from our headlamps, we'd have missed the views of the valleys, peaks in the distance, goats, sunrise on the horizon, and miles upon miles of gorgeous terrain. This ability both to zoom in *and* zoom out is crucial to a fluid and fulfilling human experience. Without the fluctuation, we miss beautiful and important things.

"Geological time includes now." It's one of my husband's favorite dad sayings, especially when we are driving through the mountains. He's referring to the fact that elements of the future world are being influenced by every current shift of the wind, every rainstorm, and every wave that crashes into a sandy beach in the here and now. These instances and their impacts may seem microcosmic and meaningless. But if you've ever noticed the rivets in solid stone created over thousands of years by the consistent flow of a downhill stream of water, then you understand. A loud, crashing waterfall is a collection of singular drops of water. The emerald color of the mountainsides in the summer are no more than a culmination of a bazillion tiny pine needles. Every singular grain of sand, on its own, seems meaningless and irrelevant. But if one grain of sand doesn't matter, then none of the rest can matter either. And if that were true, we would have no beaches. No ocean floor to hold all the drops of the ocean. And if all drops of water are without meaning or purpose, then the pine trees would never be hydrated. There would be no green moutainsides. All things contribute to the greater whole. Therefore, every drop of water and grain of sand and pine needle must matter.

Like the individual grains of sand or drops of water, every thought that runs through your mind carries some level of power within it. Each word you speak is another pine needle growing in the mountain forest. Your choices and behaviors emit influential energy that impacts yourself and other people. The way you live your life right now can and will carry on affecting things long after you are gone. Your commitment to move through this life in alignment with your most true self has the power to heal pain. It can create beauty and connection. Your pursuit of a meaning-ful life will increase the level of loving energy that exists in the world, now and potentially for generations to come.

How you think, behave, and live when your perspective is zoomed *in* colors your own experience as a human being. And it ripples out to influence other people and the world around you. Your ability to zoom *out*, consider the future and the bigger picture, and embrace your smallness within the universe will keep you humble. An expansive perspective will help you dream and remind you that hope is valuable. Know how and when to zoom in but don't forget to zoom out sometimes too. Please, have an existential crisis if you need to. Be curious about what exists beyond your limited perspective. Let your daydreams be full of wonder about what is possible. Step out of logic and embrace mystery. Because while we're doing the concrete work on ourselves and our relationships with others, remember the bigger picture matters too.

We move through life in twenty-four-hour increments, crossing things off our to-do lists, incessantly watching the time on the clock. We have conversations, hit important milestones, work, sleep, plan, and often get so lost in bulldozing through life we forget there might be a bigger point to all of it.

Meaning + Purpose

Lately, I've been thinking a lot about legacy. Our legacy is what we are remembered for. Is it egotistical or twisted that I sometimes wonder what people will say about me at my funeral someday? Considering what future generations of my bloodline will hear or understand about me makes me more conscious about the way I live my day-to-day life now. If they believe, long after I'm gone, I was hard working, is that enough? If they know I increased my net worth by a certain amount, can I be satisfied with that? Do I want the footprint I leave to be based on measurable things like money, status, material belongings, accomplishments, or credentials behind my name?

Those particular pursuits weren't doing it for me. I want my legacy to be about more. I want it to mean more. But what does "more" even look like?

As I write this, today is my mom's seventieth birthday. For the past few months, I have been collecting old photos and written messages from people who have known my mom throughout her life. I organized every picture and note into a book to give her for her birthday. I want her to have some understanding while she is still here on this Earth of her own legacy. She should know how she has affected people's lives and influenced the world around her. Going into this, I knew my mom is highly lovable and I would receive incredibly sweet messages to include in the book. However, what I had not foreseen was that nearly every single note I received reflected an obviously common thread.

Message after message rolled in telling stories of how Mom spent time with people when they were going through hard parts of life. I received stories about how she visited friends in the hospital when they were sick or hurt, how she went above and beyond when asked to help with something, and how she never failed to be a great listener when someone needed to feel heard. The range of people who contributed was wide. I received content from elementary school friends, nieces and nephews, current and past coworkers, in-laws, old neighbors, high school buddies, employers, family, and current friends. Even me and my brother's childhood daycare provider sent a message to include in the book. Their messages weren't about money, physical beauty, status, power, level of influence, or how "right" she was in any given situation. Rather, every single person wrote about how Mom had touched their lives with kindness and care.

The sheer consistency of it was shocking to me. Someday, when my mom dies, I am now confident her most talked-about and respected personal quality will be her tenacity in showing love to other humans. It won't make headlines or history books. It won't be covered on the news. But her kindness has influenced and bettered people's lives. She has made a thousand differences by making people feel seen, heard, and loved. I'm curious if perhaps something like *this* is what "more" looks like.

For the first time, maybe in my whole life, I'm coming to understand this concept more clearly. In big, bold letters stretched across the front of Mom's birthday book, I printed the word LEGACY.

My family loves to spend sacred days hiking through the Rocky Mountain aspens, fishing in alpine lakes and rivers, and sitting around campfires at night. Looking up into a billion stars against the black night sky is my favorite kind of medicine. My brother and I are both fascinated by outer space. We sit in our camp chairs staring up into the galaxies beyond galaxies, mesmerized by the infinite expansiveness of it. Considering the depth of the ocean makes me feel the same way. Sometimes, these zoomed-out perspectives of the sheer grandiosity of all things can be comforting. It reminds me that no matter how big my feelings, thoughts, or experiences feel, they all pale in comparison to the massiveness of the universe and everything in it.

But if we stay zoomed out, we lose sight of the fact that our seemingly small intentions, choices, and actions actually *do* really matter. On the most microcosmic level, even just smiling at a stranger shifts quantum vibrations and elevates the energetic frequency in the room. That's not woo-woo stuff, folks, that's science. Every loving thought, every kind act, every moment that you decide to function from a place of optimism and authenticity—it's *all* energy, and it *all* matters.

A Return to Love by Marianne Williamson is one of my all-time favorite books. She draws from *A Course in Miracles* by encouraging us to consider that a miracle can be defined as a shift in perception from fear to love. That makes us all capable of miracle making. How cool is that?! Can you imagine a world where every individual spends more time and energy on being loving to each other than we do on judging, separateness, othering (in all the neurotic ways we do that), violence, passive aggression, shaming, or any other scarcity-based thoughts and behaviors?

I recently watched a YouTube video of a postal worker who, when he delivered a family's mail each day, noticed a toddler-aged girl peeking out the window. Knowing at the time that this family was quarantined in the house for COVID-related reasons, this postal fella and little girl started a daily ritual. They danced. From outside the window, as he walked by their house to drop the mail off, he'd do a funny little move. The little girl would mimic him. Every day, when he delivered their mail, the two of them spent a few moments in playful silliness and joy with the window pane of glass between them. I can only imagine how they brightened each other's days with this small gesture.

My husband buys coffee for the next person in line at the Starbucks drive through nearly every time he goes.

In the winter, some anonymous person in the parking lot at my office spends time wiping the snow off the windshields of multiple other cars toward the end of the work day. This person stands out in the cold and delays their own commute home so the rest of us can get warm and on the road to our own homes and families a little more quickly.

My employees water my plants when I'm out of the office just because they notice it's needed.

I roll down my window and talk to the homeless people who stand on the corners of intersections around Denver asking for money. I love that they smile at me, engage in a moment of conversation, and always wish me well, even when I don't have any cash to give them.

Maybe these are the kinds of things I want my legacy to consist of.

Have you ever gotten curious enough with yourself to consider what your purpose is? Don't take your natural gifts for granted. They exist within you on purpose and for a purpose. Don't deny yourself or the world around you the blessing of the beautiful things you have to offer. And please don't make the mistake of thinking your contribution to the world needs to look like anyone else's.

We are all capable of doing better when it comes to living a purposeful life with an undercurrent of love and kindness. Don't go to your deathbed without exploring the question, "What do I want my legacy to be?" In other words, "What was the point?"

Have a point.

Live with intention.

If you are having trouble finding clarity on your purpose, start by elevating the global cumulative frequency in your own small ways by choosing love over all else. Every passing sixty seconds is a new opportunity to shift one of your negative thoughts to something more loving. Embrace every chance to do or say something kind to yourself or someone else. Every breath you take is an invitation to extend gratitude, feel the sunshine, taste the yummy food, feel your feelings, or acknowledge someone else for their beautiful contributions to your life or the world.

Your personal purpose does not have to move mountains to be profound. And your story does not have to be catastrophic or monumental to matter. Use your gifts, extend love, make meaning from your pain, and live with intention.

Be curious about the legacy you want to leave. Commit to creating an intentional footprint of some sort before you exit this world. When wondering to yourself "what's the point," have an answer.

Prior to the last ten years, most of my life was spent perfecting, predicting, and controlling everything I could possibly perfect, predict, and control. I sincerely believed my okayness was contingent on those three things being intact. I struggled with aversion to changes in expectations, for example. Heaven help the person who rerouted or ditched out on plans

Attachment versus Hope

with me at the last minute. Or, if the winter weather created dangerous driving conditions and I couldn't get to work, I would spiral into all kinds of weird emotional places. I'd feel irrationally angry at Mother Nature and shamefully worried I must be a bad employee. These anxious beliefs would leave me struggling with a restless body and racing mind. The controlling, predicting, and perfecting parts of me worked hard to curate a life and future in which surprises and uncertainties were minimal.

After years of therapy and work on myself, I now have a clear understanding around why these control-based parts were so committed to doing those jobs for me. They believed uncertainty was dangerous and led to hurt feelings, stress, and loss. They weren't necessarily wrong. Sometimes still, I feel a very real correlation between lack of control and lack of peace. Plus, these types of parts were rewarded and reinforced, further solidifying their conviction. Perfection, predictability, and a sense of control are admired, especially in our American culture. But addictions to these things will not serve us in the end. Our white-knuckle cling to them will ultimately end in more pain and disconnection.

In my midthirties, I studied concepts of Buddhism and stumbled across the notion of nonattachment. My controlling and perfecting parts did not love this. In fact, they all-out rejected it at first. At the time, I perceived nonattachment as a justification and excuse used by lazy people who didn't have life goals. I didn't want to identify with either of those things. My control-, predict-, and perfection-based parts clung to the belief that my livelihood was dependent on things going a certain way.

According to Buddhist teachings, this belief is exactly what characterizes *attachment*. Therefore, *nonattachment* can be described as a willingness to surrender control and reside in the belief that our current and future well-being is dependent on something other than the certainty of a perfected, predictable, or controllable outcome.

My therapist at the time helped me rumble with my death-grip attachment to certainty. She encouraged me to identify what was happening inside my thoughts, emotions, and body (the three buckets) when I felt a lack of control or ability to predict and perfect. She helped me realize how negatively those overfunctioning parts were affecting me. To make things even harder, the more I deconstructed my life and beliefs, and the harder I worked to shed all the crap that wasn't serving me, the more I noticed my levels of uncertainty *increasing*. That sucked. In this discomfort, I had two options: default back to the controlling and perfecting ways of my past and live with high levels of stress, ruminating thoughts, anxiety, resentment, and anger, or learn to observe my inner experience with the notion of, "Isn't that interesting?," surrender (over and over again) to this concept of nonattachment, and see if it is all the Buddhist teachings said it was cracked up to be.

Around this same time, I was introduced to *The Universe Has Your Back: Transform Fear to Faith*, a book written by Gabrielle Bernstein. I had never before correlated my attachment to control, predictability, and perfection with high levels of fear. But as I started navigating through this part of my personal transformation, it became obvious trust and faith in my own abilities to be okay and thrive, particularly in the midst of uncertainty and discomfort, had been muzzled.

Bernstein has a lot to say about fear. Through her writing, I realized the voice of fear was not *mine*. Rather, it was the voice of all my control- and perfection-based *parts*. These parts had long since hijacked the bus and been driving my thoughts, choices, and behaviors since I was a little kid. Spending more than thirty years always waiting for the next shoe to drop (and feeling like I had to be prepared for or able to predict it) was exhausting. That's an awful way to live. Bernstein's book was one of the first resources that gracefully and compassionately held my hand as I started intentionally walking straight into uncertainty instead of running away from it. It helped me come to an understanding that attachment (to things being or going a certain way) and authentic curiosity *cannot coexist*.

I wish I could say the process of expanding my own window of tolerance for uncertainty was easy and painless. But it was neither of those. When I first began to surrender to the experience of nonattachment, my feelings of stress and anxiety became way worse. The monotonous discomfort of uncertainty buzzed inside me, like a woodpecker constantly trying to tap into my thoughts, using an icepick doused in all my big emotions as its peckering beak. This was about the time I was making the choice to leave the security of a marriage, instantly decreasing my time with my children to 50 percent. I worried about whether my daughter and son would be okay, or if this choice would damage them in irreparable ways for the rest of their lives. I feared what it would feel like to go to sleep at night in a little apartment all by myself while my kids were back in my old home with their dad. I found myself in one uncomfortable conversation after another when surprised friends and family heard about my divorce and asked, "What the hell happened?" I worried about what people thought. I didn't know if I'd ever be able to become financially stable. I struggled to trust and have faith that everything would be all right ever again. My thoughts were almost completely rooted in fear. The pursuit of detachment from certainty was *so hard* and manifested in all kinds of dysregulating ways throughout that separation and divorce process. I felt like I was losing my mind. But I chose to believe in the freedom that nonattachment seemed to tout. Plus, I knew how crummy it felt to be constantly worried, and I didn't want to go back the way I had come. So I was committed to giving this nonattachment thing a go.

One year after I left my marriage, and just as I began to feel some solid ground under my feet, I finished my master's degree and made the decision to start my own private psychotherapy practice. The predictable and safe route would have been to take a job at a residential facility or treatment agency. In choosing the path of uncertainty and risk, my control-loving parts kicked and screamed in my head about financial destruction, failure, and humiliation. I remember having thoughts toward myself like, "Who do you think you are, attempting to start a business?" I didn't know if my plan would work. I believed it could. I knew it might. But I also recognized it might be a long shot. I realized that if I failed, I would have to go back to working for someone else and punching a clock while making minimum payments on multiple-thousands of dollars in new business-loan debt. To this day, I'm not sure if the choice to open a business was thoughtful and courageous, or one of my most epic life examples of igno-rance and luck. Maybe it was a little of both. Regardless, it was a testament to the practice of nonattachment.

My struggle with attachment even shows up in my recreational life. When I learned how to snowboard, I quickly got comfortable on the board when my weight was shifted into my heel side. I could rely on the strength in my quadriceps, and I had consis-tent visibility of what was downhill and in front of me. That felt controllable and safe. Unfortunately, holding all my weight in my quads for an entire ride down the mountain is not only slow but excruciatingly painful. The trick is to also get comfortable balancing your weight in your toes and against the slope of the mountain. Toe side is scary because your back is toward the downslope. Even after some level of comfort is found on the toe side, you've still gotta learn to shift between the two: heel edge of the board to toe edge, then back from toes to heels and back again as you carve down the mountain, feeling the snow under your board and relying on your body's intuition.

On a snowboard, if you don't go fast, you will fall. And falling on a snowboard is uniquely painful. It's ungraceful, and you have no time to prepare for impact. The second you get in your head and try to control too much, you're in danger. When you catch an edge, you fall hard and fast. Dip too far over to the toe edge when your front-facing side is downhill, you'll get a face full of snow and a broken wrist. Or shift back into your heels when you are facing up mountain, and you'll be flat on your ass with a bruised tailbone before you even realize you lost your balance. To stay upright, you must surrender. You learn that picking up speed is the easiest and smoothest way to transition from edge to edge. When you relax and trust your body, cruising down the mountain on a snowboard is one of the most exhilarating feelings in the whole world. The harder you fight to maintain perfect control on a board, the more you are at risk for falling and getting injured. In the true spirit of nonattachment, the more you let go and trust, the better you ride and the safer you'll be.

During the process of dismantling my relationship with attachment, I worried that nonattachment required letting go of hope. If I'm going to walk around in this life with my chest cracked open, vulnerably exposing myself to fate, did that mean I was giving up on my goals, my hopes, and the things I had been working toward? I took a giant breath of relief as I, slowly but surely, learned that no, living a life of nonattachment does *not* involve an eradication of hope. Nor does it mean we shouldn't work hard to achieve our goals and dreams.

You may continue to hope for a situation to turn out a certain way. Or hope for something to be or become true. Just stop assuming your okayness is dependent on it. Learn to be open and accepting of whatever comes to be in whatever way and whatever timing it happens. When I left my unhealthy marriage, I had zero insight about what the future held. I sometimes wondered if I would end up being alone for the rest of my life. I worried about someday perhaps regretting the decision. When I took the leap of faith to open a business, I didn't know if it was going to work. Every time I strap into my snowboard bindings, I realize there is a possibility that I will fall and get hurt.

Failure has always been a legitimate possibility. That's an inevitable part of life. Attachment says, "Be small, stay safe." It keeps us from moving beyond limiting circumstances. Hope sets its sights on a new future. I hoped that my kids would be okay through and after the divorce. I hoped I'd eventually find someone to share my life with again. I hoped my business plan would work and my private practice would succeed. And I sure hope I don't break my back on a snowboard. But since I don't own a crystal ball, nonattachment had to become my new, more sanity-saving method of survival.

My daughter Marley is trying out for the high school cheerleading team. The other night, she came home from the tryout clinic with some tears in her eyes. She said to me, "Mom, most of the kids trying out have tons of experience, so I might not make it."

She wasn't wrong. She is significantly lacking in flexibility, past experience, and certain skills that many of the other candidates bring to the table. She would be a true rookie. Not just to this team but to the sport of cheerleading itself.

I fought the urge to tell her everything would be okay. I managed to refrain from reminding her of all the ways she is incredible and totally stands a chance. Instead, I replied with, "Yep, you're right. You might get cut. How might that feel?" We had a hard conversation about disappointment, embarrassment, and sadness. We wondered what these emotions might feel like and how she'd get through them. We talked about courage. This gave me the opportunity to tell Marley about all the times I auditioned or tried out for things and got cut. Even though I eventually found my groove in the professional dance circuit, I had previously been told *no* way more times than I had heard *yes*. Knowing how much the feeling of rejection hurts, I called on empathy to meet Marley right there in the scary, dark place she was in. By the end of our talk, she began to realize her general okayness was not dependent on making this cheer team. She knew she would be able to handle the hard feelings if she got cut, even though they would really suck for a little while. She attended tryouts *hoping* to make the team, but in the true spirit of nonattachment, she now recognized she'd truly be okay if she got cut.

In circumstances when we are faced with the temptation to hold tight to attachment to a particular outcome or its timing, let's remind ourselves we can hope for things to go a certain way but ultimately, our well-being is dependent on our own capacity for tolerating and navigating through hard things. Our ability to be all right is determined by our ability to inhale, exhale, and keep waking up each day. This mentality of nonattachment relies on an understanding that okayness is a gradient range, not a static state of being. We might be sad or angry or scared or grieving, or we might be sick or injured or unemployed or broke or alone. None of those things have the power to take your ultimate okayness away from you. If you can breathe and if your heart is beating, then you are at least some level of okay. Don't forget that.

Keep hoping. Just begin to release the death grip on control. Let's let go of certainty and attachment to things being a certain way. Hold the elements and pursuits in your life in an open hand, not a closed fist. Introduce this new perspective about nonattachment to your control-based parts and give them permission to relax a little bit. As they begin to ease up, the release will allow a natural stream of curiosity to enter in. Consider the bigger picture. Throughout the infinite, expansive universe; the depths of the oceans; the grandiosity of nature; and the history of all time that has passed before this moment right now, billions of things have happened in spite of attempts to predict, perfect, or control them. If you have faith in anything bigger than yourself, don't bypass the part where we trust that thing's ultimate power. Build and sharpen that faith by releasing your attachment and beginning to believe that everything will truly be okay, one way or another.

Joy and gratitude are inextricably connected. I don't believe one can exist without the presence of the other. These are things that can be practiced, muscles that can be exercised. You have all the power in the world to multiply the amount of joy you experience. Increasing the number of moments that involve the element of joy is a privilege, and arguably one of the most sacred assignments of this lifetime.

Joy

In the fall of 1997, I was nineteen years old and a freshman at the University of Kansas. Naismith Hall was the coed dorm at the bottom of the hill, toward the edge of campus. Across the street was Oliver Hall, another residential building. Well past my bedtime on a school night in early November, I was sitting at my desk doing homework and watching the first snow of the season fall from the sky. Big, fat flakes had been coming down hard for a few hours. I had lived my whole life in Kansas and knew all too well the misery of Midwest winters. The walk up the hill to my early classes the next morning was going to be gray, wet, windy, and bitterly cold.

With at least an hour of homework left to finish before I could close my eyes and sleep, I heard a ruckus outside. From my eighth-floor window, I could see a crowd of students down on the ground. At midnight on a Tuesday, these crazy asses were outside playing in the snow! I felt as curious as I did annoyed. My roommate and I threw on our coats and decided to go see what the late-night, outside shenanigans were all about.

Room 824, where we lived, faced away from the street. So it wasn't until we got to the ground level that we saw the same chaos was breaking loose across the street at Oliver. At least one hundred kids were down there, catching snowflakes on their tongues, making snow angels, and constructing massive fort walls. A group on each side of the street was busy making snowballs. We made it down there just in time to see the kick-off of an epic snowball battle between Naismith and Oliver Halls.

I struck up a conversation with a couple students I recognized from the Naismith cafeteria. I can't remember where they said they were from. But I will never forget the awe in their faces as they told me they had never seen snow before. These eighteen-, nineteen-, and twenty-year-old students were running and diving in the snow like children. They forgot how to feel the cold and lost themselves in the play of the snowball fight. Their joy was contagious. After nearly two decades of living in it, I had experienced enough of the icy roads and the relentless months of cold, gray Kansas winter skies to form a conviction to move away from the state as soon as I graduated from KU. I was jaded by the frigid, wet weather. But these first-timers made me momentarily forget my bias. They helped me remember the joy of playing in it.

I laid down on my back in the snow and watched the white flakes fall from the dark sky. It was hypnotizing, like traveling through a galaxy of stars. I felt wonderment at the orange, hazy weirdness of the sky caused by the streetlights reflecting off the low snow clouds. I was remembering how to be a kid. The recognition of that playful, childlike joy felt like medicine to my stressed-out, agenda-saturated spirit. Joy is a simple thing. It doesn't require a productive outcome or logic of any kind. When my roommate and I finally went back up to our room, it was 2 a.m. We fell into our beds exhausted, with red cheeks, cold toes, and joy-filled hearts.

Decades later, that's still a memory that stays tucked away in my mind until the first snow of each winter. I remember the images and the sounds, and I refeel the joy.

I once heard the perspective that our cells have ears. They listen to every thought in our mind in search of direction on how to function. Negative, scarcity-based thoughts tell our cells that things are not okay, that *we* are not okay. Then our cells react accordingly. We see empirical evidence of this all the time in research done on the relationship between negative thinking and physical ailments such as cancer, autoimmune disorders, digestive issues, and cardiovascular disease. On the flip side, thoughts rooted in joyful abundance tell every cell in our body that we are okay and this life is worth living. They respond accordingly to this, too, by boosting our immune system, elevating our personal vibration, and contributing to the cumulative positive frequency of the people and world around us.

In our society, there exists a giant myth that joy and happiness must be correlated. Joy certainly exists when we are happy, but I don't believe happiness is required in order to experience joy. Here's the difference: happiness is an emotional side effect of our hopes or expectations being met or surpassed. It is more charged than contentment but less so than ecstasy. Happy is just one of our many emotions. But joy is something else.

Joy is, of course, a positive internal experience, but it is more than an emotion. It has a spiritual energy and a cognitive element to it too. Joy can be a byproduct, but it can also be an intentional choice. The experience of joy is a signal we have our finger on the pulse of something real. Something that moves us. Alignment. Conversely, a noticeable lack of joy is a telltale sign we are *out* of alignment. Interestingly and perhaps surprisingly, happiness is not a mandatory ingredient for joy. My very favorite thing about joy is that its existence is not dependent on circumstance. Joy exists even in the darkest experiences, in the hardest of moments.

I want to be careful here not to dip over into a Little Miss Sunshine soapbox about how you should look on the bright side and find the silver lining in all situations. It can be potentially damaging to brush the reality of pain and struggle under the rug. So let's not do that. Instead, can we agree that *both* can be present at the same time: pain and joy?

Pain, in varying degrees ranging from discomfort to outright misery, is inevitable. But it is possible to stay tethered to alignment even during horrific turmoil. Think of a moment in your life when you remember experiencing tremendous distress, perhaps even agony. When you capture that snapshot in your mind, do you remember it as holistically awful? If so, I challenge you to look again and try to see some small shimmer of gratitude.

On Friday, June 6th, 2014, I was boarding a flight from Denver to Kansas City to visit Matt for the weekend. He was my boyfriend at the time, and we were dating long-distance. Per the norm, everyone boarding the flight stayed in their own little bubbles with their faces lit up by the glowing screens of their phones. With ten feet more to walk before stepping from the jetway onto the plane, my phone rang. It was my mom. An intuitive knowingness hit fast and hard. The walls of the jetway started closing in on me. Before I answered the call, I knew my dad was dead.

He had been in a nursing home with round-the-clock care for the past eight months. His body had been slowly shutting down for years. In the end, alcohol-induced dementia took his life. His mind had been functioning much like someone with Alzheimer's, forgetting more and more of himself and his life by the week. Decades of alcohol use had pickled and trashed his brain and internal organs. His spirit was tired, and his body could no longer sustain beyond the damage.

I had visited my dad on Wednesday, two days prior. Before I left, I helped him to move from his bed to the commons area so he could eat dinner. As I waited for the elevator doors to open at the nursing home that evening, I looked back at him sitting at a small table by himself, dousing his food in green Tabasco sauce.

I think I knew, as I stepped into the elevator, that this glance would be the last time I saw my dad alive.

So when my mom called two days later, I caught my breath. I answered. She said my dad was gone and told me to get on the plane and go to Kansas City to be with Matt. As I hung up the phone, time and space stopped being real. My knees buckled. Someone grabbed me so I wouldn't fall. I felt someone else ease my backpack off my shoulders. I collapsed into some stranger's lap and sobbed.

Nobody complained that the boarding process had stopped. Nobody tried to push past us. The whole jetway of people paused to grieve with me. Everything was quiet except for the noise of agony coming out of my throat and sniffles from a few other folks on the jetway who were joining me in some tears.

After confirming I still wanted to fly, they helped me onto the plane and put my carry-on luggage away for me. After takeoff, a flight attendant brought me a cold beer and a note written on a napkin. It was a message of condolence signed by both pilots and the flight crew. I cried quietly in my seat for the entirety of the seventy-five-minute flight, feeling like I had floated out of my body.

Let's rewind. Two years prior to my dad's death, I started my divorce process. The intervening twenty-four months were the hardest of my life. I walked away from a husband, home, and dog that I deeply loved. I learned to be away from my children 50 percent of the time. I quit my salaried job in exchange for a ten-month, full-time, unpaid internship, finished the home stretch of graduate school, was one year into launching a private psychotherapy practice, and was simultaneously watching my dad slowly die. I was broke, overwhelmed, often scared, and sometimes really lonely. As a survival mechanism, I decided to integrate an active gratitude practice into my life. The discipline of this practice was my lifeline. It was my oxygen tank.

I would toggle between different thirty-day gratitude challenges. One month, I would wake up and write down three things I felt grateful for. The next month, I would post one thing per day on social media that brought me joy. On most days, it was nothing profound. I would write down or post about how the coffee shop nailed my three-pump, half-caff, no-dairy, iced, vanilla latte perfectly, or how grateful I was I had finished my grad school homework in time to watch thirty minutes of brainless television before I needed to go to bed. I would put a gratitude post on Instagram with a photo of my daughter after losing her first tooth, or a picture of my beat-to-shit favorite slippers that continued to hang on even as the seams tore out. I wrote or posted about anything that brought me an ounce of comfort, a touch of hope, or a moment of relief from the chaos and turmoil of my life. The small, daily gestures added up. This gratitude practice kept my head above water, sometimes just enough so that I could inhale tiny sips of air. Without this tether to joy, I believe depression and anxiety would have pulled me under.

Fast forward to 2014. Nothing prepared me for the pain of getting that phone call on the jetway that day. I had known for many years that my dad would not live a long life. He was sixty-six when he died, thirty years (to the day) older than me. But logic and understanding don't stand a chance against grief. Grief takes you out. It is one of the only emotions that leaves no room for rationale. It is a completely *felt* experience. For me, it was like someone punched a hole in my stomach, reached up into my heart, and tore part of it off. I still feel the pain of it. I probably always will.

And also...joy.

That day on the plane when my world fell apart, I had access to joy. Even as I crumpled to the floor, feeling like I might never get my legs back under me again, I felt joy in the form of gratitude that someone had thought to take my heavy backpack off my shoulders before I collapsed. Joy was there in the comforting presence of a total stranger sitting with me on the floor of a jetway while I fell apart in their lap. Even through the haze of tears and a visceral knowledge that everyone was looking at me while I boarded the plane, I could feel a tiny thread of gratitude for my cotravelers' patience. This flight full of strangers was feeling *with* me. I was able to notice the joy because I was prepared for this moment. Not because I was ready to lose my dad, but because I had practiced feeling joy and gratitude every day for the last two years. My system knew how to find it, how to feel it, regardless of how dark any moment or experience seemed. I had done it so many times as part of a discipline that the feeling of joy was right there ready to serve as my lifeline, even when the tsunami of sadness threatened to swallow me up. I was open to the love of others because I had practiced being open. I was well-exercised at looking for joy in the darkness.

I don't know your story. I don't know your hardships. There are many unimaginable circumstances I can't even begin to wrap my head and heart around. I've not struggled with infertility or years of unrelenting physical angst from a long battle with cancer or autoimmune disease. I've never lost a limb, fought in a war, or filed for bankruptcy. I don't know the soul-crushing agony of miscarriage or losing a child. I've never lived on the street or been without clean food and water. So I cannot claim to know your pain, whatever it might be, because I have not walked in your shoes.

Even though I don't intimately know the depth or intensity of your pain, I do believe opportunities for you to feel joy are possible. But you must be willing to seek them out. Even the most pitch-dark room can no longer be experienced as a completely black space if one tiny candle is lit. I am sorry you have experienced great pain. My heart bleeds with yours, not because I know exactly what you have been through, but because I know struggle. I know fear and overwhelm. I know rejection. I know loss. I know insecurity. I know what it feels like to consider that ending my own life might be the best idea for myself and everyone else. If you were collapsing under the weight of this world in front of me right now, I would hold you in my arms and let you fall apart in my lap. I may not know you, but I know what it is to be human. It is vulnerable. It is really hard. As you cried in my arms, I would allow myself to feel my own pain so I could be with you in yours. In that shared experience of awfulness, you and I would both feel a sliver of joy.

Connection does that. It holds space for all the complexity and all the feels.

We don't fight like crazy to notice joy in order to get a gold star or because it will make the pain go away. Neither of those things will happen. Rather, we do it because it changes the experience. It shifts the psychological, emotional, and physiological climate within us. Intentionally being curious enough to wonder about and seek joy is a choice, a hard and terribly intimate and vulnerable one. But we do it anyway because joy is medicine. It reminds us of who we are when the temptation to be pulled into a space of negativity and hopelessness threatens to pull us completely away from our line of alignment.

What if joy is the whole point? Or maybe connection is the whole point, and joy is one of the main tools used to achieve an ultimately connected, loving existence. What if the willingness to try and access joy, especially in the most dark and awful of experiences, is necessary for living in alignment? Perhaps it serves as a barometer for whether we are on track with that pursuit or not. If I was an all-knowing and all-powerful, magical wizard and I told you that the intentional pursuit to know, find, and feel joy was the key to an aligned life full of abundance, would you try it? Better yet, would you chase it?

Take an inventory of your life thus far. If you could chart every minute out on a spreadsheet, then put a checkmark next to each one in which you experienced joy, would the overall average of the minutes of your life be accompanied by a checkmark? Or would they be without? What about over the last month? Or the last week? Or the past hour? If too many minutes stand naked and alone without a checkmark next to them, that's a sign that either your joy muscles could use some exercise or some significant life shift needs to happen so joy isn't quite so hard to find.

Doesn't it make sense that an intention to live more minutes than not in a space of joy would ultimately accumulate to a really fulfilling life? It would not be a life without struggle because that does not exist. Rather, it would be a fascinating tapestry with multicolored fabrics interwoven with a brilliantly shining, sparkly thread where joy has been present. If that is what it means to be fully yourself, fully human, and fully alive and to do so while staying tethered to all things related to connection and love, okay then. Count me in. In this, a cumulative common effort, we will never be alone. I do hope you will join me.

U-turns and question marks are wielded by the courageous. They elicit an awake life. A bold life. By using mindful introspection and curiosity, you sign a contract with yourself to nonjudgmentally observe whatever you discover inside yourself, in other people, and throughout the world around you. It requires a bold promise to advocate for all the younger, past versions of

Conclusion

yourself. The process requires forgiveness, self-compassion, and a tenacious dedication to your future self and the pursuit of connection. In an existence in which you will inevitably become well-acquainted with pain and struggle, living in alignment with your integrity, values, and purpose becomes the new North Star.

Change is natural and necessary. You aren't meant to stay the same year after year, decade after decade. "Do the best you can until you know better," Maya Angelou once famously said, "then when you know better, do better." It's a battle cry, a fight against complacency. This invitation into brave exploration is a call to challenge what you think you know. I recognize your attachment to certainty as an attempt to feel safe because, me too. I understand the craving to cement your feet into a convicted set of beliefs or familiar behaviors. I know the temptation to stay, even when your gut instinct says to go. I have felt the fear of immeasurable uncertainty. The risks of failure, being wrong, or making others uncomfortable or upset are unsettling, and at times excruciating.

Ask yourself: do you believe you are the best version of yourself when you *feel* like yourself? Do you acknowledge you have gifts to share with the people and world around you? To embrace the pursuit of continuous personal evolution is to realize *there is no finish line*. It is a conviction to stop playing broken records and be open to changing the narrative over and over again, whenever necessary, until the end of time. It means we choose connection over competition in spite of our differences. It requires we consciously opt for compassion over point proving, listening over talking, and integrity over blame shifting, grudge holding, excuse making, or shame.

Certainty plus static conviction do *not* equate to a thriving livelihood. Curiosity, compassion, and connection, however? Yes. *This*. This is the combination that will move the trajectory of human okayness up and to the right.

It is time. Look inward and inquire. Mindfully observe what happens in your mind, heart, and body. Don't run away from hard feelings. Feel them, fully. Know your bricks. Show up for curious conversations with the parts of you that overfunction and block the energy of your most authentic Self. Honor and respect your parts' attempts to protect and help you. Collaborate with and lead your parts in the process of creating purposeful and meaningful change in the areas of your life where your integrity and alignment are out of whack.

Look straight into the eyes of others, truly *see* them, and use more question marks than periods. Try on perspectives that are not your own. Be willing to be wrong, and embrace the call to change your mind when necessary so you can grow. Stand by your boundaries and protect your integrity. Be okay with the fact that you will not be everyone's cup of tea. Choose love again and again and again.

Believe in something bigger than yourself. Stay hopeful but nonattached to any specific outcome or timing. Look for joy in all phases of life and in every moment.

Trust yourself. You are equipped. When you fall short, you may fall flat on your face. Don't be afraid to open your eyes and look around while you are down there. It's the only opportunity to get to know that particular perspective. Then stand back up, dust yourself off, and get back to the admirable business of making U-turns and using more question marks. Whatever you do, don't settle for anything less than an exceptional life full of curiosity.

The reins are in your hands now. Evolve or repeat, people.

Evolve or repeat.

Evolve.

I spent the first weekend of December 2019 in Austin, Texas, with my editorial team, wrangling my thoughts and ideas into the skeleton of this, my first book. While in Austin, I became so sick with a respiratory virus that I refused to sleep at night out of fear I might stop breathing. In hindsight, I should have gone to the hospital. Although it would be a few more months before I knew

Acknowledgments

what COVID-19 was, I'm certain this was the first way the virus touched the writing of this book.

The year 2020 was supposed to be a time of calm, a year of relaxed routine. It was slated as my year to focus, write, edit, complete, and publish *More Your-SELF*. The Universe had other plans. On Friday the thirteenth, as COVID-19 shut the world down, my time and energy began to become stretched to the point of near transparency, like thin, wispy spindles of cotton candy, in more directions than I could count.

I answered the demand in the mental health industry by taking on as many clients as I could handle. Through my speaking business, I virtually supported corporate organizations, nonprofits, and school districts as they learned to provide their employees, members, and parents with psychological wellness tools during that very unfamiliar, uncertain, and scary time. When schools closed, we turned our dining room table into a remote education station for our children and tried our darndest to contribute with some parental guidance in their schooling in the sparse minutes between meetings, webinars, and virtual client sessions. Finally, I recorded and produced a nineteen-episode, interview-based podcast season in the attempt to spread the power of interpersonal connection during a moment in history when disconnection rose to a toxic and heavy, ultimate high.

I explain this not to elicit your kudos or sympathy. Rather, I need it to be understood how vital the support of my people was in continuing and eventually completing this book. My writing had to happen in the hours after client sessions, after podcast recordings, after helping the kids with schoolwork, after the speaking gigs, when I was exhausted, burned out, and sometimes wanting to give up. I kept my head above water, just barely at times, and continued to write one page after the next because my tribe held me up and kept me from going under. Without them, this project would have been dead in the water just months after it got started.

Thank you to my team at Scribe Media. Emily Gindlesparger, Hal Clifford, and Tucker Max, your confidence in my content and encouragement to put it into the world got this thing off the ground. Thank you for reminding me that my voice matters. To my author cohort and community, thank you for making me excited about writing. Special thanks to Molly Gimmel and Nika Kabiri for keeping me honest and accountable to weekly progress. Katie Villalobos, my publishing manager, you are the best bowling-lane bumpers I could have asked for, guiding me through the process and across the finish line. I had no idea how complex the editing process was until my team of editors raked through my manuscript multiple times over, helping me fine-tune the content and filter out unnecessary fluff. Charity Young, Jessica Findley, Zoe Ratches, and Callie Barringer, thank you for your sharp eyes and helpful feedback. Rikki Jump, you were my first Scribe contact at the very beginning. Thank you for saying yes and later for the marketing guidance. Anna Dorfman, thank you for my beautiful cover. Scribe Media and Lioncrest Publishing, big love for being by my side from the first words on the screen, all the way to getting pages between covers, sitting on bookstore shelves.

To every single one of the hundreds of clients I've worked with over the years, I want you to know how much you've inspired me. You've shown a kind of courage I've not seen anywhere else during my lifetime. Thank you for trusting me with your vulnerability and teaching me what it looks like to voluntarily step into uncertainty and extreme discomfort for the ultimate betterment of oneself, the people we love, and the world around us. You will never fully know how much each of you have blessed and influenced my life.

Thanks to my crazy-makers. You know who you are (and, let's be honest, will likely never read my book). You have provided me with opportunities to question what I think I know in order to practice empathy, perspective taking, and boundary setting. The manifestations of your dysfunction have prompted me to rumble with my own integrity. Our difficult interactions and experiences together have been the breeding ground for much of my best personal evolution. Thank you for initiating the opportunity for me to at times challenge and change my mind about an outdated behavior or way of thinking. I respect the value of those hard parts of my life and your roles in them.

I say all the time that if you want to be a lion, you gotta run with the lions. I am surrounded by a *beast* of a network and community. There ain't no way this thing would have ever happened if it weren't for my people supporting the effort, holding space for me throughout the roller coaster of a ride, and nudging me forward one paragraph at a time.

When I say I run with the lions, I'm talking about the fiercest of the fierce. My girlfriends are fucking mountain lions. We run in packs, supporting, protecting, and empowering each other. The women in my life are a *force*. They are truth-seekers and pattern breakers out doing their thing in the world in ways that inspire me to no end. Their hugs have melted me into a puddle when I've been so at the end of my rope that I couldn't stand on my own two feet. Our dancing, singing, stargazing, yoga-ing, mountain biking, hiking, laugh-until-we-pee-our-pants hang times always rejuvenate me. Abbe—the loyal friend, fellow adventurer, grief companion, and soul sister. Kelsi, KK, and Kimmy—the Wild + Free. Holly and Kristin—my way-back women, who've been along for the ride for twenty-five years and provide a steady undercurrent of love and creativity, always. The Denver Broncos Cheerleaders alumni—the ultimate examples of women supporting and empowering other women. Thank you, all, for the love and conversations that provoked and extracted so much of this book's content from my mind and heart.

To my Aunt Judy, whose life ended during the last week of the writing of this book. Thank you for loving people so ferociously. Not just people who looked, believed, and lived life just like you, but *all* people. You've been teaching me by example how to love people well since the day I was born. I can't wait for the day we are all together again on the other side.

To Doug. Your mom goes to college.

Rooney, my ride-or-die. You were the first person who listened to my book idea, and, without thinking for longer than a few seconds, you told me, "Yes, do this." Just like all the other times you believed in me more than I sometimes believed in myself, you were not about to let me fail on this project. Thank you for reminding me of my power and my purpose when I struggle to remember them for myself.

It is a terribly vulnerable thing to let someone else share pieces of your own story. To my ex-husband Sean, thank you for trusting me with a glimpse into one of the hardest parts of our lives. I recognize the courage involved in doing so, and I'm grateful.

Mom, your encouragement to speak my truth, even when others don't understand it or it pisses people off, has been my pilot light while writing this book. Over the past couple decades, you and I have both learned a lot about what it means to be authentic. Do no harm, but take no shit. Thank you for reminding me that I'm a good human, especially when my voice is unpopular with someone who isn't grounded in their own okayness enough to receive it. You are the OG of my fan club and the best role model, friend, and mother I could have ever dreamed of having. I know we, as mothers, sometimes wonder if we've done a good enough job, if we've done right by our kids. I am certain that I speak for both Casey and myself when I say *yes*, 100 percent. Emphatically and unequivocally. As far as moms go, we got the best one.

Dad, wherever you are in the cosmic ethers, I know you contributed to getting this book into the world. I wish I'd better known the value of curiosity when you were still alive. My side of our conversations would have been overflowing with question marks rather than periods. I would have fought so much harder to hear and understand your story. I'm sorry I didn't. I feel you all the time. I know you are with me. I hope you know I understand why things were the way they were. And I know the YOU that was buried under the layers of pain and protective parts. So much of who I am comes from you. I love you, and I miss you so much. Save me a seat.

My brother's hugs have the power to heal pain and comfort fear. They are the best in the whole world. And the laughter that is an inevitable part of almost every one of our interactions has been medicine for me so many times over the past few years. Casey, thank you for loving me. Thank you for following me to Colorado all those years ago, enabling us to live this life in tandem. I cannot imagine not having you and your family nearby. There is a room full of love in my heart that has, does, and will forever be reserved for you and you alone.

Marley and Beckham, my babies. The loves of my life. Thank you for believing in me. Thank you for understanding and giving me grace when I've had to miss games, events, ski seasons, and school holiday parties. You have no idea how much it has meant to me when you've given me kisses on the cheek and said, "I love you, mom," while my face was buried in the computer screen.

Or when you've quietly laid down next to me on the sofa, just to share space while I write. I promise to stay committed to my own personal evolution so I can show up for you as my truest and best Self. My heart beats for the two of you. I love you 3000.

My Matthew. My person. I've felt no greater adoration and companionship in my life than that which you've shown me. I have letters written by you when we were nineteen years old encouraging me to do what feels true and most authentic, even when it would ultimately lead to your own broken heart. You've always been my most unrelenting champion. Thank you for the many years of extending the utmost curiosity in my direction. Thank you for working to know and understand my whole system of parts and believing that behind their walls of protection is a Self worth giving your whole heart to. I will forever be honored to share your time, your space, and your last name. You are my safest place. This book would absolutely not exist without you.

Printed in the USA
CPSIA information can be obtained
at www.ICGtesting.com
LVHW041340200923
758757LV00014BA/44/J